Men and Women Serving Jesus and His Church

Jim Estep, David Roadcup, Gary Johnson

e2

effectiveelders

Scripture quotes in this work come from the New International Version, New American Standard Bible and English Standard Version. In the following text they will be indicated, respectively, as (NIV), (NASB) and (ESV).

ISBN 978-0-578-66617-4
www.e2elders.org

Cover design by Gary Gogis / www.gogisdesign.com

Foreword

Doug Crozier
CEO, The Solomon Foundation

There is always a lure that catches people's attention and draws them into attending a local church for the first time. It may be a neighbor, a holiday event; for me it was a preschool program. It was the late 1980s and my wife and I and our two young daughters were living in Mission Viejo, CA. We had moved from the east coast in late 1986 and the first thing my wife did was look for a preschool. The local Chamber of Commerce recommended the preschool at Mission Viejo Christian Church (MVCC). We were fortunate to get our two girls into the preschool and we began attending MVCC. My wife Julie and I had grown up in the Methodist church and had been sprinkled. We studied Scripture and the church took us through an exceptional process to fully understand the meaning of baptism by immersion. In early 1987 we were baptized and became members of MVCC. Being washed by the water as adults, we were taught the importance of immersion; it transformed our lives and ultimately the outcome. We fully understood the commitment we were making in becoming Christians, and we were full of joy!

The years carried on, Julie and I were faithful in our attendance and study of the Word, which led to the leadership of MVCC inviting me to be a deacon. I was honored and very interested in getting more involved; I loved our church! My biggest hurdle to overcome was the lack of a detailed training process to become a deacon. I studied Scripture, specifically 1 Timothy 3:8-13. I felt like I was prepared but I really wasn't. Looking back, I wish I had more resources to study and learn about church leadership, including becoming a deacon. There are many resources on church leadership, including the work and role of elders, but much less for deacons.

I wish I would have had *#DeaconStrong* in my tool chest as a young deacon all those years ago. Thankfully you can! What a great resource for a young leader looking to serve, but more importantly, to be able to fully understand what they are signing up for! The four parts of this book outline the basics:

- Part 1 gives the biblical understanding of being a deacon. The definition, the qualifications question of women serving as deacons lays a foundation.
- Part 2 dives into the historical perspective which I found fascinating. I enjoyed the chapter on deacons in the Restoration Movement. I am very strong supporter of our movement and found it fascinating to read the perspectives of men like Stone, Campbell and others.
- Part 3 speaks into the relational considerations for deacons; how deacons work with Elders, Staff – and within their own family.
- Part 4 covers the practical side of deacons – selecting, equipping and assessing deacons.

Never forget how powerful the lure of a good children's program can be. It not only led us to MVCC, but also led me to leadership roles in the church. I was surrounded by men of great faith, Mac McElroy, our senior pastor at MVCC, Elders like Bill Black, Doug Hastings, Dave Bowman, Everett Sallee and Jerry Briggs. They helped develop my servant leader skills as a deacon. A short time after being asked to be a deacon, I was asked to become an Elder, and later, Chairman of the Elders during a time of great growth at MVCC. These men also helped me through the struggles of life, the celebrations of life and all the ups and downs in between.

Eventually I ended up where I am today, leading a rapidly growing church extension fund. We currently partner with over 300 churches and I am personally encouraging them all to provide this resource to their leaders.

If you start a leader well by providing them resources like *#DeaconStrong* and encourage them through the process, they will grow to become a pillar of strength in the church. Strong leaders make strong churches. We all want strong, vibrant churches, so be sure to invest in your leaders!

Thank you, Gary, David and Jim, for your thoughtful and thorough research and writing on this key subject of deacons!

Table of Contents

Introduction

Countless lives were changed at 2:49pm on April 15, 2013. Three people were killed, more than a dozen individuals lost limbs and hundreds of people were injured when two pressure-cooker bombs detonated. In the hours and days that followed, still more individuals would be wounded and killed as the manhunt proceeded for the Tsarnaev brothers, those alleged to have perpetrated the crime.

The 117th running of the Boston Marathon will never be forgotten because of this terrorist act and for the indescribable pain it caused; but moreover, it will also be remembered for the movement that was birthed in the days following the tragedy.

Immediately after the blasts, the people of Boston became united – and in a powerful way. Many hotels near the blast zone were closed, leaving guests in the city suddenly without lodging. Yet, just as suddenly, Bostonians opened their homes to these strangers from afar. Moreover, law enforcement officials began calling on the general public to help them identify and locate the Tsarnaev brothers, whose images had been captured by cameras as they each carried bomb-laden backpacks towards the area of the marathon's finish line. Hundreds – even thousands – of pieces of information flooded police and FBI offices. As a result, both brothers were quickly located by law enforcement. As well, the medical community responded with rapid and expert care for the myriad of people injured. And still, hundreds of thousands of dollars began pouring in from tens of thousands of people to meet the immediate needs of bombing victims. Contributions flowed into Boston from across the country and around the world. All said, we watched as #BostonStrong became a reality.

Though two brothers sought to destroy life and limb, a movement intensified in the days following that it continues to grow; a movement that you and I now immediately recognize as #____Strong. This idea has become a battle cry response when tragedy strikes. From coast to coast and even the world over, this phrase is immediately recognizable. Yet, it is more than a mantra; it has become a movement. To be "strong" is an intentional resolve of people to help people. It is a hope-filled lifestyle of helping others.

For centuries since its birth, the Church has relied on people to help people. Jesus "did not come to be served, but to serve, and to give His life as a ransom for many" (Mk. 10:45 NIV). "Whoever claims to live in Him must live as Jesus did" (1 John 2:6 NIV). Hence, we are resolved to serve, to help others. We, the Church, are committed to a hope-filled lifestyle of helping others. We are ***#DeaconStrong: Men and Women Serving Jesus and His Church.***

This book is focused on the role of deacons serving the local church, and it is our intent to help these individuals serve more effectively and enjoyably. To that end, we have written this book in four sections, from four complementary viewpoints.

Biblical Understanding

First, we *look into* Scripture to gain an accurate understanding of the word and work of a "deacon." We discover the qualifications of deacons and address the issue of women serving as deacons. This first section is essential as we want to clear up confusion surrounding this important role in the local church.

Historical Perspective

Second, we *look back* historically to the role of deacon in the Restoration Movement, to the advent of the Church Board to govern the church, and to a return of deacons serving within a polity of elder governance as shown in the book of Acts.

Relational Considerations

Third, we *look around* at the relationships in a deacon's life. They do not serve in a vacuum. Deacons are not an island onto themselves. Deacons serve alongside people. They do life in relationship with elders, with staff, and most importantly, with their families. Healthy deacons can foster healthy relationships, and healthy relationships create a healthier church.

Practical Applications

Finally, we *look ahead* and apply our deacon-related discoveries from our study to future deacon-related initiatives we must pursue, such as selecting deacons, equipping deacons and assessing deacons. With minds to understand the times (1 Chron. 12:32), we share what the local church must do in practical terms to help deacons excel in their role.

To Be Stronger

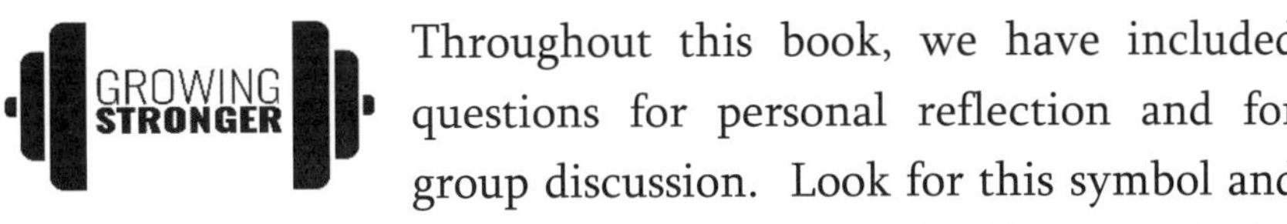

Throughout this book, we have included questions for personal reflection and for group discussion. Look for this symbol and pause for the express purpose to think and talk through the information you just read. Engage one another. Ponder how to personally apply what you are reading and learning. Grow stronger.

Introduction

These days are urgent. People all around us need help for today and hope for tomorrow. And the local church will make all the difference, particularly when we are ***#DeaconStrong: Men and Women Serving Jesus and His Church.***

Part 1: Biblical Understanding

Chapter 1: The Definition of Deacon

David Roadcup

Walking into my home church on Sunday morning, I witness a beautiful sight. There are people deeply involved in serving the body of Christ here in Burlington, Kentucky. There are people preparing communion, serving in the nursery and children's ministry area. People are welcoming visitors, preparing to lead worship musically, making coffee and doing many other forms of important ministry in Jesus' name. The picture of people serving others is pure gold. It is beautiful. It is how our Lord planned for the body to be enriched and nurtured. These wonderful people were called into service and are serving well, giving themselves away in Jesus name!

The early church's term for many of these people I see on Sunday morning was "deacon." From studying Scripture, we know the Greek word διακον (English "deacon") always meant "someone who serves." It described or identified a servant, a helper, an attendant, an assistant, a waiter or a minister – someone who sees needs and meets them, someone who willingly puts themselves into the service of others. Greek experts Liddell and Scott tell us that the root meaning of this word *deacon*, meant "for someone to reach out with diligence to render service on behalf of others."[1]

The service of well-trained and functioning deacons is a critical part of a healthy church body! When desiring to build an effective church, the role of the deacon is indispensable. As deacons are trained, set aside, prayed for and then released to do

[1] Liddell and Scott, *Greek-English Lexicon* (Oxford University, 1871), 369.

their ministries, the church grows, meets needs and is able to fulfill its mission. An effective team of deacons is essential to any church's forward movement!

The New Testament Definition

Scripture describes deacons as a group of believers who are involved in serving the church. Scripture is clear about deacons: who they should be, what they do and how they are to fulfill their ministry mission. The base Greek word in the New Testament is *diákonos* (διακονος). This word primarily meant "servant." The person in the New Testament referred to as a "deacon" literally was to serve others. The word is also translated "helper," "waiting-man," "minister," and "messenger." Commentaries are of divided opinion, but one possible origin of the word could come from two different Greek words that meant "through" and "dust;" therefore, these servants "kick up dust by getting things done."[2] Whether this specific etymology is accurate or not, their role as depicted in the New Testament is an active role, focused on service and ministry.

There are three general forms of the word.

Greek	English	Speech Part	Short Definition	Freq.
διακονεω	diakoneo	verb	to minister	37
διακονια	diakonia	noun	the work/ministry of	34
διακονος	diakonos	noun	servant/minister	29

[2] Contrast Charles Hodge. *God's Deacons* (Star Bible and Tract Corporation, 1979), 13 with Strong's Entry under Thayer's Greek Lexicon on https://biblehub.com/greek/1249.htm. This and all subsequent footnoted internet links accessed February 17th to 28th, 2020 unless indicated.

It is the last word, *diakonos*, which became Anglicized as "deacon" via Latin.[3] [4]

Today and formerly, the word has often been used to denote an office. However, this word is better used to describe a function or ministry – that of *servant*. Therefore, we will most often use the translation "servant" in this book (at times "lead servant" and "servant leader"), instead of the transliteration "deacon."

In light of this need in the life of every church, God created the ministry of the servant. God specifically called people into the identifiable role of being asked to serve in specific ways. This is clearly seen in Acts 6:1-7 where, apparently, the first "lead servants" were identified and ordained through prayer and the laying on of hands (v. 6). While the personal noun *diakonos* is not used in Acts 6, it is easy to see that these men were called to do the work of serving and meeting needs in the life of the early church, and the function/role noun form, *diakonia*, does occur twice in these verses, along with the verb, *diakoneo*, once. Paul goes on in 1 Timothy 3:8-13 to name the position and identify the qualifications necessary to fulfill this ministry function.

A Deacon is Defined by Following Jesus' Example

Just as the word indicates, a deacon is defined by service, work and ministry. Jesus is our greatest example when it comes to

---

[3] J. Stephen Sandifer. *Deacons: Male and Female: A Study for Churches of Christ* (Self Published, 1989), 15.

[4] For more information regarding these three Greek words, see:
Diakoneo: https://biblehub.com/greek/1247.htm
Diakonia: https://biblehub.com/greek/1248.htm
Diakonos: https://biblehub.com/greek/1249.htm

serving others. During His entire public ministry, Jesus was teaching the masses, casting out demons, healing and feeding people and ushering in the Kingdom of God. His life was truly, in every way, a life of "deaconing" – serving – among us. Jesus told us that was why He came. In Matthew 20:25-28, He taught the disciples a key lesson about serving in a spirit of humility.

> *But Jesus called them to Himself and said, "You know that the rulers of the Gentiles lord it over them, and their great men exercise authority over them. It is not this way among you, but whoever wishes to become great among you shall be your servant, and whoever wishes to be first among you shall be your slave; just as the Son of Man did not come to be served, but to serve, and to give His life a ransom for many."* (NASB)

(The companion texts to Matthew 20:25-28 are Mark 10:41-45, Luke 22:24-27 and John 13:12-17.)

In the time of Christ, the privileged did not serve those beneath them. Those beneath served those above. Throughout all of history, this has been the template. In this passage, Jesus taught the disciples that they are called, not to be served but to serve, following His example. This concept was totally foreign to those of Jesus' day – and to us! Jesus initiated a complete counter-cultural perspective when He told the disciples that greatness in the Kingdom of God is found in serving others, not in being served. We must see that Jesus changed the equation here. He created a new template. The economy of the Kingdom of God tells us that as servants of Jesus, we find true greatness through service and humility. This is what He expected from the Twelve and what He expects from us today.

One of the things I love about Jesus is that He never asks us to do anything that He is not first willing to do Himself. He commanded us to serve and then immediately modeled for us what He asks us to do. *That* is a truly excellent leader.

One of the greatest examples of Jesus serving others came on the night that He celebrated His last Passover with the disciples.

This story is very familiar to many of us. Jesus was facing the Garden of Gethsemane and Judas' betrayal. He knew an illegal trial and conviction awaited Him. He would face the cross in a few hours. Just prior to these events, Jesus and His disciples were in the upper room celebrating the Passover meal together. In the week before this event, the Gospel writers tell us that the disciples were engaged in intense debates about who was the greatest among them. This disagreement continued throughout the week, right up and even into the Passover meal! Luke specifically wrote that even during dinner, the disciples were having this … "discussion" (Lk. 22:24).

At a certain point in the meal, the record tells us that Jesus got up from the table, laid aside His outer garment, girded Himself with a towel, poured water into a basin and knelt down by each disciple and washed their feet. What a powerful moment in Jesus' relationship to the disciples!

Jesus our Lord, the King and Creator of the universe, washed their feet! The Master over life and death, demonic forces, nature and time, Lord of eternity, knelt over a bucket of dirty water as a lowly servant and washed His followers' feet. Imagine the shock when they began to realize what was about to happen, and then over the many minutes that followed, *as* it happened! "No, this cannot be taking place!" they must have thought. But Jesus, wanting them to understand an important lesson they had not yet internalized, proceeded to, one by one, wash their feet. As mentioned, we must understand that in the Jewish or Gentile culture of the day, this simply was not done! But Jesus did things all the time that were not expected by those around Him. He washed their feet, one at a time, all twenty-four feet, all one hundred and twenty toes! Peter was the only one to verbalize and request that Jesus not wash his feet (the others were almost certainly thinking what Peter said). John recorded that immediately upon finishing the task, Jesus put aside the towel and basin and initiated one of the most impacting teachings imparted to the disciples in all of their years together.

> *So when He had washed their feet, and taken His garments and reclined at the table again, He said to them, "Do you know what I have done to you? You call Me Teacher and Lord; and you are right, for so I am. If I then, the Lord and the Teacher, washed your feet, you also ought to wash one another's feet. For I gave you an example that you also should do as I did to you. Truly, truly, I say to you, a slave is not greater than his master, nor is one who is sent greater than the one who sent him. If you know these things, you are blessed if you do them.*
>
> *John 13:12-17* (NASB)

In His comments after the foot washing, Jesus drove home the lesson implicit in this powerful, informal teaching opportunity. He shared several specific points.

In verse 12, Jesus, using a rhetorical question, asked, "Do you know what I have done to you?" He wanted them to think deeply about His action of washing their feet. "Do you understand the meaning of what just happened to you?" Jesus was asking them to ponder this powerful Kingdom lesson about humility. He wanted them to understand that serving others with a spirit of humility is the key to Christian leadership and ministry.

In verses 13-15, Jesus reinforced the truth that He was and is, indeed, their Lord and Teacher. As their leader, washing their feet, they, therefore, were to wash each other's feet. "I gave you an example that you also should do as I did to you." Jesus led them, not with words only, but by the way of His powerful life. He told them what He had just showed them – they were to serve similarly and follow His lead.

In verse 13, He told the disciples that the key to fulfilling what they just witnessed comes when they do what they have just witnessed. They were not to discuss, in a small group, the lesson Jesus taught. They were not to merely listen to someone remind them about it when they gathered in the future on a Sunday morning. They were to put action into His directive. They had to follow His example by serving one another. He reminded them – and us – that if this lesson is planted deeply in believers' hearts and minds, they won't just talk about serving but will actually put hands to the task and boots on the ground to accomplish His request. Jesus declared that we will be blessed as we live out the servant lifestyle, modeled by our Lord Himself. This entire scene is a powerful, profound and defining moment with the disciples.

As a servant – a deacon – in the body of Christ, we follow the example of our Lord and we "wash feet." We do this through serving the church as we effectively accomplish our requested tasks and ministry. There are many places for service in the Lord's Church. It may entail leading a team of believers in Guest Services, Community Outreach, Small Group Ministry or using our teaching gift. We may use our gifts of administration, mercy, hospitality or compassionately ministering to the elderly. We may be asked to help with the organization of preparing and serving the Lord's Supper, baptisms or youth ministry. We may change dirty diapers in the nursery every week. There are multiple areas of service important to keeping the church healthy, effective and moving toward the fruitfulness that the Lord has planned for us.

A Deacon is Defined by Serving from the Heart

A servant's ministry should come from the fact that he knows and loves Jesus with his whole heart. When we come to Christ through faith and experience our baptisms, our lives are to be cut in two. Our hearts and minds are dramatically changed. Our changed hearts reflect the fact that we have left the old life behind and are enjoying and growing in our new life in Christ. Several elements are involved in this action. We surrender our hearts. We purify them before the Lord each day. We guard our hearts and do not allow anything unclean or impure to invade them. Our service to Jesus and His Church must come from our heartfelt expressions of affection, compassion and dedication to Him as the only Lord and Savior. This has to be the foundation from which our ministry comes.

Performing acts of service out of any other motive should not take place. We have been redeemed; we are grateful for all the Lord has done in our lives. We respond with our time, effort, focus and work as effective servants – deacons – of the church of Jesus Christ.

As a servant in the church, we have an opportunity to partner with God in strengthening His Church by helping her fulfill her mission. We are coworkers with our Heavenly Father. What a privilege! What an honor!

Scripture is clear about the value of an effective servant. Paul declared that "those who have served well as [servants] obtain for themselves a high standing and great confidence in the faith that is in Christ Jesus" (1 Tim. 3:13, NASB). A dedicated servant who knows his assignment and does his work with excellence is of "high standing" in the Lord's sight. God greatly values servants who "deacon" well.

How should we define "deacon?" Deacons are servants, ministers, dedicated workers in God's kingdom who fulfill their callings by loving, ministering to and serving the people of God who make up the body of Christ. Serve well, my friends, and glorify the Lord through your work.

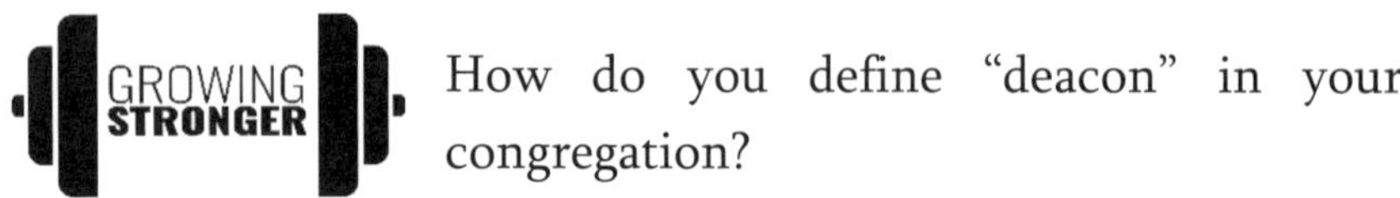

How do you define "deacon" in your congregation?

Is this understanding explicit (written down in a governing document) or implicit (an "unwritten rule")?

Does this chapter challenge your understanding? If so, how?

Chapter 2: Qualifications of Deacons

David Roadcup

Therefore, brethren, select from among you seven men of good reputation, full of the Spirit and of wisdom, whom we may put in charge of this task.
Acts 6:3 (NASB)

Whatever you do, do your work heartily, as for the Lord rather than for men, knowing that from the Lord you will receive the reward of the inheritance. It is the Lord Christ whom you serve.
Colossians 3:23-24 (NASB)

Bob was a growing Christ follower who had never been directly involved in the ministries of the church he attended. He and his family went to services each Sunday, contributed financially and were emotionally connected but not involved. Bob and Kay decided to join a small group. The group they joined was led by one of the elders in the church. The elder soon discovered that Bob was a very successful project manager in a large firm. He identified the fact that Bob had excellent management gifts and was very effective at leading his team at work. Bob was approached about stepping into the role of lead servant in their congregation. He accepted, went through the training requested by the elders, began his new position and became one of the most effective servants in the church. He accepted the role of leading the Missions Team and led that team to a new level of effectiveness and ministry.

The role of servant is a vital role of important ministry! Lead Servants oversee the day-to-day, boots-on-the-ground work of the church. They lead the church's ministries. They are vital to the health and growth of their congregations.

Being qualified for a job or position is critical to the success of accomplishing that assignment. Being qualified means that a person is officially recognized as being ready to tackle a particular assignment. It means that a person is certified, competent and knowledgeable in having the ability to perform a task or execute a job.

Scripture tells us that there are definitive qualifications for servants who lead ministries. There are two places in the New Testament that list specific qualifications. We want to examine the qualifications given by the early church leaders and explain and apply them for those who desire this ministry.

The Biblical Qualifications of Servants

The first grouping of qualifications comes in Acts 6:3, with the surrounding text of Acts 6:1-7 detailing the circumstances that prompted their selection. The appointing of servants here sprang from a very practical need. Greek widows in Jerusalem were missed in daily food distribution. As a result, the Apostles (elders) asked the Greek believers to choose seven men from among them who would lead this important ministry.

We should note that the Apostles did not decide to divide up the names of Greek widows and begin making food deliveries themselves. They clearly understood that they were called to a specific ministry and should not have been prevented from doing it (v. 4). So other servants – deacons – were chosen and appointed to service. We should recognize that this move on the Apostles' part was good leadership. Good leaders bring others into their ministries. Effective leaders also understand the importance of identifying ministry priorities. The Apostles had their ministry priorities well-aligned. Feeding the Greek widows was important. The Apostles managed the situation well. They did not leave their first role (ministering the Word and prayer), while they also organized a qualified team of servants to meet the additional need.

The first group of qualifications lists three items (depending on your translation of choice). We will consider three, as given in the NASB's rendering of the verse: 1) men of good reputation, 2) full of the Spirit, and 3) men of wisdom.

First, "good reputation" refers to men who were, back then, and, today, known for their integrity and honesty. They are solid and dependable. Their word is their bond. They have a good reputation within the church, in their families and outside in the social and business communities where they live and work. Their reputations extend into the neighborhoods where they live. As men of good reputation go about their daily lives, they will become known for their integrity and purity. These are the kind of believers who will make effective servants.

Second, "full of the Spirit" teaches that these men are to be filled with the Holy Spirit of God. They know the Lord. They walk in the Holy Spirit every day. They are men who live a daily Christ-like life and who have the mind of Jesus in all things. They live and minister as Jesus would have lived and ministered. The fruit of the Spirit (Gal. 5:22-23) is part of their nature due to their deep and personal conversion to Christ.

Understand also that the phrase "full of the Spirit" can easily be misinterpreted.

> *Some commentators think this refers to "spiritual gifts and miraculous powers," but there are certain*

> *objections to this opinion. We have had no account thus far of any except the apostles having received the miraculous power from the Spirit – so the historian Luke cannot be fairly understood as referring, by this expression, to such powers. "Full of the Spirit" must then mean "full of the fruit of the Spirit" as respects a holy life.*[5]

Third, "full of wisdom" indicates that a potential servant will be someone who allows Scripture to guide him in all decisions, morals, values and discernment. The word for wisdom in this passage, *sophias* (σοφιας) in the Greek, meant "insight, skill or intelligence." Men of wisdom exhibit careful thought and express a deep well of insight when it comes to making decisions. When a decision needs to be made, the person who possesses this trait will always go to Scripture and prayer before making the decision or choosing a path. Gareth Reese, in his excellent commentary on Acts states, "The idea (of wisdom) seems to be prudence, or skill, to be able to make a wise and equitable distribution so as to give no offense in their ministrations."[6]

The second grouping of qualifications is listed in 1 Timothy 3:8-13. Paul, writing to Timothy (and vicariously to all subsequent church leaders), identifies eight more qualifications to be considered when choosing servants. Let's examine each of these.

Men of Dignity (v. 8): This term normally refers to something that is honorable, esteemed, or worthy, and is closely related to "respectable." The NIV translates this as "worthy of respect." A lead servant is someone known, appreciated and respected by the

---

[5] J.W. McGarvey, *Original Commentary on Acts* (Christian Classics Ethereal Library, 1892), 105.
[6] Gareth Reese. *Acts* (College Press, 1976), 251.

congregation. His witness and heart are exemplified by his Christian walk. This qualification is also given as a qualification for elders (1 Tim. 3:2).

Not double-tongued (v. 8): J. Stephen Sandifer gives an excellent explanation of the phrase from the Greek for "not double-tongued;" (*may dilogos*, μη διλογους). Pointing out this is the only use of this word in the New Testament, he explains, "The literal meaning is 'not (ma) two (di) words (logos).' The deacon does not say one thing to one person, and another thing to someone else. Current slang would say that a deacon should not speak out of both sides of his mouth."[7] A servant-leader must always be a believer who lives a life of truth-telling. He must be someone who is a truthful person. Lying and/or misdirection have no place in the life of a Christ-follower, especially one that is presented to the congregation as a servant leader.

Not addicted to much wine (v. 8): The literal translation of these words directs that a believer partakes in "not much wine." Responsible translations indicate that the deacon is not to be "given to much wine" and "not given to wine." The use of alcoholic beverages by church leaders must be carefully managed. A good servant-leader is someone who is temperate when it comes to alcohol. Alexander Strauch wrote:

> *Note carefully that Paul actually says, "...not addicted (given to)* much *wine" (emphasis added). Plainly this is not an absolute prohibition against drinking wine. It is a prohibition against the abuse*

---

[7] J. Stephen Sandifer. *Deacons Male and Female? A Study For Churches of Christ* (Keystone Publishing, 1989), 47.

> *of wine (or any other substance) that would damage a man's testimony and work for God.*[8]

The consumption of alcoholic beverages must be handled in a temperate way and managed carefully by those who lead ministries. Drunkenness and excess would be reason for one to step down from his servant leader responsibilities. Moderation is absolutely necessary for the sake of witness and example.

Not fond of sordid gain (v. 8): The presence of greed (the extreme desire for money and possessions) has been with people from the beginning. It was a pressing problem during the time of Jesus with those who bought and sold in the Temple. Jesus strongly criticized the religious leaders of His day in Luke 11:39 and 20:47 for their excessive greed and love of money. Even one of his closest followers, Judas, robbed the disciples' monetary resource on a regular basis (Jn. 12:6). Paul also wrote about greed when discussing the false teachers of his day, "Judiazers," who repeatedly tried to destroy the churches he had planted. Paul certainly had these wolves in mind when he wrote 1 Timothy 6:5 and Titus 1:11. The importance of understanding the strong lure of greed should be on the "radar screens" of all believers, especially of those who are leading the church. "Deacons handle money – other people's money, the church's money – and where money is there are always problems. Money is an irresistible magnet for many people."[9]

A person desiring a servant's ministry should search his heart, be aware of this temptation and be sure it is under control in his life.

---

[8] Alexander Strauch. *Minister of Mercy-The New Testament Deacon* (Lewis and Roth Publishers, 1992), 98.
[9] Ibid, 99.

A potential servant who does not have this area in check should delay his pursuit of this important ministry.

Holding to the mystery of the faith with a clear conscience (v. 9): The phrase "the mystery of the faith" is just one way Paul speaks of the Gospel (compare to 1 Tim. 3:16). Consequently, this statement refers to the need for servants to hold firmly to the Word of Truth without wavering. False doctrine abounds in our day without question. Yet this qualification does not merely involve one's beliefs, for he must also hold these beliefs "with a clear conscience." That is, the behavior of a servant must be consistent with his beliefs. This is "eyes-wide-open" belief and conviction, not begrudging assent.

Tested ... [and] beyond reproach (v. 10): "Blameless" or "beyond reproach" is a general term referring to a person's overall character. Although Paul does not specify what type of testing is to take place, at a minimum, the candidate's personal integrity, personal purity, overall reputation, and theological positions should be examined. Moreover, the elders should not only examine a potential servant's moral, spiritual, and doctrinal maturity, but should also consider their track record of service in the church. This is a different Greek word than was used in verse two during Paul's discussion of elders/overseers.[10]

Husband of one wife (v. 12): The best interpretation of this difficult phrase is to understand it as referring to the faithfulness of a husband toward his wife. The most literal rendition would be "a one-woman man." That is, there must be no other woman in his life to whom he relates in an intimate way either

---

[10] Verse 2: https://biblehub.com/greek/423.htm
Verse 10: https://biblehub.com/greek/410.htm

emotionally or physically.[11] In contrast to "beyond reproach," this phrase is the same Greek phrase used of elders in verse two.

Good manager of their children and household (v. 12): A servant must be the spiritual high priest of his home and leader of his wife and children. In Paul's discussion of this for *elder* qualifications, he poses a question: if an elder cannot control and manage his household, how can he manage the household of God (1 Tim. 3:4-5)? Men desiring the role of servant should love their wives sacrificially, discipline and train their children, and manage their household affairs with care.

Paul's Statement About Women in 1 Tim. 3:11

In this qualifications section, Paul gives an exhortation to women. He writes, "Women must likewise be dignified, not malicious gossips, but temperate, faithful in all things" (NASB). The Greek word here for "woman" is *guna* (γυνη῾, "goo-nay"). It is used throughout the New Testament interchangeably as "woman" or "wife." The identity of these women is thoroughly discussed in the following chapter.

Another word about terminology: the New Testament does not, in fact, use the term "deaconess." Only the word *deacon* occurs and it is grammatically masculine; however, as a descriptive title it is used to describe both men and women, e.g. Phoebe is called a deacon in Romans 16:1. Using the word "deaconess" is a linguistic accommodation regarding women who are servants as opposed to men who are servants, should the need for distinction arise.

---

[11] Limited space does not allow for an extensive discussion on this important topic. For further study, see Alexander Strauch, *The New Testament Deacon*, Chapter 8 and/or Estep-Roadcup-Johnson, *Answer His Call*, Appendix 4.

In verse 11, *guna* could also mean simply "women" in a broader sense. Nothing in the text nor context would preclude women who are single or widowed from being servants of the church. In Romans 16:1, Paul writes, "I commend to you our sister Phoebe, who is a servant (διακονον) of the church which is at Cenchrea." Phoebe is clearly identified as a servant, indeed *deacon*, in this context. Married women, single and widowed women, can be servants, according to New Testament teaching. A thorough study of both 1 Timothy 3:11 and Romans 16:1 is undertaken in the following chapter of this work.

For the purposes of this chapter about a servant's qualifications, we should consider Paul's directions given here to women/wives. He enumerates four concepts.

Women (wives) should be dignified. Similarly to what is described above from verse eight regarding servants, wives, widows and single women are to be honorable, respectable and esteemed when desiring to be servant in the church.

Not malicious gossips: Paul encourages women and/or wives to exercise restraint, being careful in their conversations, not to gossip. Their conversations should reflect the Lord. Women are not to participate in gossip, slander, jealousy or bitterness when talking to others. Malicious gossips are dangerous as they can bring disunity and brokenness to relationships, or even to an entire church. Godly women do not participate in this type of sin. Leviticus 19:16 and Proverbs 10:18 (among other Scriptures) strictly prohibit gossiping among God's people of either gender.

Sober minded: This concept in the Greek describes a woman who is self-controlled, strong in character, speech and conduct. It also refers to the ideas of having balanced judgement and being free from debilitating excesses.

Faithful in all things: The Greek words used in this phrase are beautiful words. The word "faithful" carries the idea of loyalty, being trustworthy, reliable or dependable. The phrase would describe a woman who is a person of high integrity and strength; one who lives a holy life.

The qualifications given in Scripture about men and women serving the church are necessary to study and important to continue building into one's life, irrespective of role or station in the congregation. They all mirror the attitudes and lifestyles expected of a person who lives like Jesus and follows in His steps. It may take time to mature each of these qualifications in one's life. We are all on a growing journey of spiritual learning, awareness and discipline. Keep moving forward. Keep growing. Our Father is patient. He will lovingly move you forward as you seek to serve Him through your ministry and service.

Which four qualifications do you most readily reflect?

Which four qualifications do you need to work on to improve your reflection?

How can your process for vetting potential deacons incorporate these qualifications even more effectively?

Chapter 3: Women as Deacons

Jim Estep

What do we do with the women mentioned in 1 Timothy 3:11? We cannot just skip the verse; we cannot pretend it's not there, leaving the matter wholly unaddressed.

> *Their [guna] likewise must be dignified, not slanderers, but sober-minded, faithful in all things. Let deacons each be the husband of one [guna], managing their children and their own households well. For those who serve well as deacons gain a good standing for themselves and also great confidence in the faith that is in Christ Jesus.*
>
> *1 Timothy 3:11-13* (ESV)

What's a "*guna?*" It is the first Greek word (γυνἠ, "goo-nay") in what is now verse 11 of 1 Timothy chapter 3. Its Greek meaning was interchangeably either woman or wife, the specific translation of which depended entirely on context alone. There are no spelling differences, differences of accent or declension. Please remember this word, because to avoid confusion throughout the chapter, I'll use it – "*guna*" – when addressing the biblical passage so as to avoid unintentional biasing.

The Greek text of 1 Timothy 3:11 is absent of any definite article (the) or possessive pronoun (their) before *guna*. "The" or "their" is added by several popular English translations. The verse simply starts, "*Guna* likewise…" Translations are, in fact, fairly evenly divided. In short, a clear translation of the first phrase of 3:11 would be most accurately rendered: "Women / Wives likewise…" There is no "the" or "their" in the Greek. Here is a chart of eight

English translations depicting their uses of "women" or "wives," indicating use or non-use of an article, in this verse:

Translation	Word	"The"	"Their"
Holman Christian Standard Bible (HCSB)	Wives	–	–
New Living Translation (NLT)	Wives		✓
English Standard Version (ESV)	Wives		✓
King James Version (KJV)	Wives		✓
New International Version (NIV)	Women	✓	
New American Standard Bible (NASB)	Women	–	–
American Standard Version (ASV)	Women	–	–
Revised Standard Version (RSV)	Women	✓	

Translation is always, to some extent, an art, and Jerome's Latin Vulgate translates the Greek *guna* in 1 Timothy 3:11 as Latin's *mulieres*, which can be "woman" or "wife," similarly to Greek. But unlike Greek, wife and woman do have different words in Latin, *uxorem* and *mulieres* respectively; therefore, Jerome opted not to use the word that would exclusively mean "wife."

In light of this topic, we must also remember Romans 16:1-2 (ESV):

> *I commend to you our sister Phoebe, a [deacon] of the church at Cenchraeae, that you may welcome her in the Lord in a way worthy of the saints, and help her in whatever she may need from you, for she has been a patron of many and of myself as well.*

Paul here introduces us to Phoebe, directly describing her as a deacon – a servant. "Deacon" is a descriptive term of function, the gender about whom it is used is of little to no importance.[12]

---

[12] James Hope Moulton and George Milligan, *A Greek-English Lexicon of the New Testament and Other Early Christian Literature* (Eerdmans Publishing, 1976), 184-185.

Who were these Women?

Who were the *guna* in 1 Timothy 3:11? In order to provide an accurate interpretation, whoever they are must be explained in the context of the church's lead ministry servants, since servants – deacons – are the topic of the verses immediately prior to and following verse 11. To suggest otherwise would violate not only every hermeneutical principle but also common sense. Several possibilities have been articulated regarding the *guna* of 1 Timothy 3:11[13] and we will now consider those possibilities.

Christian Women in General? Maybe the *guna* are just "women." This is a broadly suggested interpretation and it is equally as broad in its application. Are we not all to be servants, including women? Indeed, we are. However, does this relate to the immediate context? It would make little sense to discuss overseers, then servants, then introduce a general instruction to all women, then return to servants as a focused topic. Hence, this interpretation has never been the most widely accepted.

Widows? Could the *guna* be the widows mentioned in 1 Timothy 5:9-10?[14] If that was Paul's intended meaning here in chapter 3, why didn't he just use the word for widow (*chera,* χερα) as he did in chapter 5, rather than *guna*? Widows are more likely to be those who receive ministry from servants than those

---

[13] Compare Blackburn, 303-310; Gareth L. Reese, *New Testament Epistles: 1 Timothy, Titus, 2 Timothy* (Moberly, Missouri: Scripture Exposition Books, 1999), 140-141; Sandifer, 33-44; Alexander Strauch, *Paul's Vision for the Deacons* (Littleton, Colorado: Lewis and Roth Publishers, 2017), 121-123, 155-170; Jennifer H. Stiefel, "Women Deacons in 1 Timothy: A Linguistic and Literary Look at 'Women Likewise…' (1 Tim. 3:11), "*New Testament Studies* (Vol. 41, 1995): 451-456.

[14] M.H. Shepherd Jr., "Deaconess," *The Interpreter's Dictionary of the Bible* (Nashville: Abingdon Press, 1969), Volume 1, 786.

actively doing the ministry[15] – and that is precisely what happened in Acts 6:1-7.

Women Helpers to the Deacons? Some see these *guna* as deacon assistants, since the word "helper" (Greek *prostatis,* προστατις) is used of Phoebe in Romans 16:2 (rendered "patron" in ESV). However, as with the previous two interpretations, this one simply doesn't have a lot of credence, nor even context. Romans 16:2 is the only use of *prostatis* in the entire New Testament. Given the broader context of 1 Timothy 3:8-13, this understanding of being helpers would seem to belong *after* Paul's description of deacons, not dead center in the middle of his discussion of them.

Wives of Deacons and Elders? Could *guna* qualifications apply to the wives of both the elders and deacons? This interpretation could be more highly regarded if, as above, verse 11 followed the list of qualifications for servant, applicable to both elders and deacons, but it's not. Paul wrote about elders, deacons, *guna*, and then went back to deacons. This interpretation – that *guna* indicates only the wives of elders and servants, but cannot be elders nor servants themselves – would be more palatable if Paul had written about elders, deacons, *guna,* and then stopped. But he didn't. He mentions them within his discussion of servants, so whoever these *guna* are, they must be tied to the idea of lead servant more directly.

Wives of Deacons? Could the *guna* in verse 11 be the wives of servants, but not servants themselves, nor wives of elders? If this is the case, we must note that similar qualifications are never given for elders' wives in any of Paul's writing; hence the idea of the servant's wife having qualifications would lend itself to

[15] Van Dam, 118.

servants being either men or women – husbands and/or their wives. If these are qualifications for the wives of lead servants merely because they are their wives, then why didn't Paul dictate similar qualifications for wives of elders, who are of a "higher" role in the church's leadership? Being that verse 11 is in the middle of the text regarding qualifications of servants, one practical observation is that, perhaps, the wives of servants were to serve alongside their husbands; perhaps individuals were not so much appointed to service, but couples were jointly appointed. This may be demonstrated by the fact that the wives of servants have qualifications, whereas the wives of elders do not have explicit qualifications. However, again, the New Testament uses *deacon* as a role and function descriptor, not as a gender-dependent title like "chairman" or "chairwoman."

Women Deacons? Could the *guna* be servants who are women? Perhaps this final interpretation is the simplest. Once again, this is not the office of "deaconess," which does not appear in Scripture. Rather, this understanding is the function and role of *servant* being fulfilled by women. Candidly, this is the more obvious, plain meaning, but is not free from question.

Some draw a distinction between being a deacon/servant, and being in the diaconate, i.e. an official body of "designated servants." In such discussions, Phoebe is often assumed to be the former, but not included in the latter. However, this seems to be more of an interpretive bias by high church exegetes accustomed to considering the role more formally and officially. They often will separate early references to servants (Acts 6 being around 32 AD) from later references (Philippians 1, 1 Timothy 3, both probably in the late-60s AD) for this reason. An additional reason to set aside deacon-diaconate as a false dichotomy is the recognition that the *guna* are getting equal attention in terms of qualification. The word "likewise" is used in both verses 8 and 11, paralleling the two, i.e. both of these statements by Paul are laying out a servant's qualifications. When Paul wrote this letter to the preacher at Ephesus, he gave instructions about those *serving* and described expectations of them, some of whom were women – that is, women deacons.

In sum of these six possibilities, the latter two interpretations have the most validity, with women simply being deacons having the fewest exegetical concerns. Because of the biblical testimony, we should affirm women servants, whether we take the position that this means the wives of servants who are serving jointly with their husbands as couples, or we understand this as being women placed in the role and function of lead servant.

Did the Church Have Women Deacons?

While perhaps unfamiliar to many contemporary congregations, women lead servants, or "deaconesses," are present throughout the history of Christianity. The early church created the term. In 112 AD, with the Church under persecution, Governor Pliny the Younger sent a letter to Emperor Trajan with this insight:

> *Accordingly, I judged it all the more necessary to find out what the truth was by torturing two female slaves who were called ministrae.*[16]

Ministrae is the Latin equivalent to *diakonoi*, which is a plural form of the personal noun *diakonos*.

---

[16] Pliny, *Letters*, 10: 96-97; https://faculty.georgetown.edu/jod/texts/pliny.html; see also Blackburn, 314; and the Vulgate translation of Romans 16:1.

A number of women's tombstones from the early church were engraved with διακονος, e.g. Sophia, the deacon.[17] As early as the 3rd century AD the Syrian *Didascalia Apostolorum*, Chapter 16, "On the appointment of Deacons and Deaconesses," explained their value in ministry, "especially needful and important," particularly to other women.[18] However, debate started to occur in the 4th century AD.[19]

Women deacons historically have had a place in the older church traditions, such as the Roman Catholic, Byzantine and Orthodox churches.[20] Likewise, women deacons were present throughout various traditions in the Reformation.[21] While some may be tempted to dismiss the place of women lead servants as a matter for only the high churches, they are present in virtually all Protestant traditions. For example, the European Baptist tradition historically has accepted women servants, though the majority of Baptist churches in the United States do not.[22] But what about the Restoration Movement?

---

17 Elizabeth A. McCabe, "A Reevaluation of Phoebe in Romans 16:1-2 as a *Diakonos* and *Prostatis*: Exposing the Inaccuracies of English Translations," *Women in the Biblical World* (New York: University Press of America, 2009), 100-101.

18 http://www.earlychristianwritings.com/text/didascalia.html, Feb. 17, 2020.

19 Barry L. Blackburn, "The Identity of the 'Women' in 1 Tim. 3:11," *Essays on Woman in Earliest Christianity, Volume 1* (Joplin, MO: College Press, 1993), 303.

20 Phyllis Zagano, *Women Deacons? Essays and Answers* (Collegeville, Minnesota: Liturgical Press, 2016); Gary Macy, *Women Deacons: Past, Present, Future* (Mahwah, NJ: Paulist Press, 2011).

21 Sandifer, 99-107; Cornelis Van Dam, *The Deacon: Biblical Foundations for Today's Ministry of Mercy* (Grand Rapids: Reformed Heritage Books, 2016), 115-130.

22 Charles W. Deweese, *Women Deacons and Deaconesses: 400 Years of Baptist Service* (Macon, Georgia: Mercer University Press, 2005).

Did the Restoration Movement have Women Deacons?

There is no dispute that the churches of the early Restoration Movement valued and affirmed women lead servants, often called "deaconesses." Alexander Campbell notes that "Amongst the Greeks who paid so much regard to differences of sex, female deacons, or deaconesses, were appointed to visit and wait upon the sisters," noting "Phebe [sic] of Cenchrea, and other persons mentioned in the New Testament, who labored in the gospel."[23] Similarly, W. K. Pendleton in 1848 wrote "Besides deacons, every church should have deaconesses, whose duty it is to perform such offices as cannot be so well performed by deacons, and especially such to females, as could not with delicacy and propriety be laid upon the deacons."[24] In his pivotal series on permanent offices in the church, Robert Milligan in 1855 wrote, "The Phebes [sic] [i.e., women deacons] should, therefore, constitute a part of the διακονοι [deacons] of every fully organized Christian congregation,"[25] which included ministering to "the feeble, the sick, the poor, and the destitute, especially of their own sex."[26] Notice that Milligan did not limit female servants only to ministry to other women; he simply noted their particular advantage to ministering among women.

The most comprehensive study on the subject of deacons in the Restoration Movement was completed by J. Stephen Sandifer,

---

[23] Alexander Campbell, "A Restoration of the Ancient Order of Things. No. XIX. The Deacon's Office," *Christian Baptist*, 1826 (reprinted 1983), 335.
[24] W. K. Pendleton, "Deacons – Should the Church Have Them," *Millennial Harbinger* (1870): 54.
[25] Robert Milligan, "The Permanent Orders of the Christian Ministry," *Millennial Harbinger* (1855): 626.
[26] Milligan, 626.

who wrote *Deacons: Male and Female – A Study for the Churches of Christ* (1989). It traces the existence of women lead servants in all three main divisions of the Restoration Movement; a capella, independent, and Disciples; well into the 20th century. For example, in 1932, Standard published R. C. Harding's *Handbook for Elders and Deacons*, which stated emphatically, "It seems clear from the Scriptures that there must have been a least some of the churches with female servants or deacons," citing Romans 16:1, 1 Timothy, and their presence in early Christian sources.[27] Likewise, Herbert E. Winkler published *The Eldership* in 1950, dedicating an entire chapter to affirming the biblical presence of "Deaconesses;" its subsequent chapter "Should We Have Deaconesses Today?" argued pragmatically of the necessity of mobilizing the majority of our church members – women – and the unimaginable results of failing to so do.[28]

So, Why the Objection to Women Deacons?

While it is true that now the a capella Churches of Christ and Christian Churches / Churches of Christ typically do not have women lead servants, it has not always been the case. From our Movement's inception, the early leaders of the Restoration Movement affirmed and valued women deacons or deaconesses. Why the change? Why did the Restoration Movement seem to remove women servants? There are several reasons which contribute to varying and overlapping degrees.

---

[27] R. C. Harding, *Handbook for Elders and Deacons* (Cincinnati: Standard Publishing, 1932), 95.

[28] Herbert E. Winkler, *The Eldership* (Nashville, Tennessee: Williams Printing Company, 1950), 169-179, 180-182 respectively.

"Deaconesses are not biblical!" The perennial question for any believer is, "Do we have a text?" The term deaconess does not occur in the pages of the New Testament – it is true. Many individuals reject the notion of women servants by noting that we hear nothing of deaconesses in the New Testament. Agreed, but this is an argument from semantics.[29] No one suggests that the early church had elders, evangelists, deacons and deaconesses, a fourth and separately identified role. (Again, we simply note that servants were male or female. Paul calls Phoebe a deacon, not a deaconess.[30])

The question here is about women servants, whether they are servant-leaders themselves or "merely" the wives of ministry leaders, serving alongside their husbands. The notion of women servants is plainly present in the New Testament in at least both 1 Timothy 3 and Romans 16. It is additionally possible in Philippians as some have speculated about Euodia and Syntyche being deacons in light of Paul's addressing of his letter to "overseers and [servants]" in Philippians 1:1, combined with his direct address of these two women in Philippians 4:2. One commentator observed, "Critics frequently object that the Scriptures do not say much about female deacons. Those critics should be reminded that the Scriptures do not say much about the male deacons either. It is scholastically dangerous to be dogmatic about either sex in the diaconal role in the first century."[31] In sum, one factor for the gradual erosion of the woman lead servant was this semantic debate.

---

[29] See James D. Bales, *The Deacon and His Work* (Shreveport, Louisiana: Lambert Book House, 1967), 75-79.
[30] Aheto Sema, "Phoebe: Deacon or Deaconess," *Bible Translation* (April 2009): 106-111.
[31] Sandifer, 41.

The Divergence of the Restoration Movement In 1906, the Restoration Movement began to splinter into what has now emerged as the right / a capella, centrist / Independent, and left / Disciples. This division continued throughout the early and mid-century, culminating in the 1960s. As this split progressed, the Disciples retained women servants, and have them even today. The a capella churches moved away from appointing "deaconesses," and the centrists divided over the issue, but with time leaned toward their a capella brethren.

Likewise, geography played a role. The more progressive Disciples of Christ gravitated toward the north and tended to affirm women deacons. The more conservative south tended to slowly remove women servants.[32] However, the presence of women servants was not the catalyst for the division of the Restoration Movement; it was, rather, a casualty of the division.

The Influence of J. W. McGarvey In the late 19th and early 20th centuries, one of the most significant voices in the Restoration Movement, one that opposed the advent of liberalism among what would eventually become the Disciples of Christ, was J. W. McGarvey. Part of our a capella brethren, he was a preacher, professor, and author. In two *Christian Standard* articles of 1902 and 1906, he voiced opposition to the notion of deaconesses / women servants in general.[33] His voice carried weight not only among the a capella churches, but into instrumental Christian Churches as well. While others directly opposed his opinion, few had the reputation or influence of McGarvey. Even Philip Y. Pendleton, tasked with completing

---

[32] Sandifer, 167-171.

[33] J. W. McGarvey, "Deaconnesses," *Christian Standard* (November 22, 1902): 1616; "Deaconnesses," *Christian Standard* (February 3, 1916): 166.

McGarvey's unfinished Standard commentary on Romans following his death, opposed McGarvey's opinion. Commenting on Romans 16:1, he noted "The word 'deaconess' is found only here; but this single reference with commendation stamps the office with apostolic sanction and approval."[34] However, McGarvey's opinion has continued echoing even to the present.

Women's Suffrage Movement The pace of social and cultural changes at the turn of the 20th century was staggering. Unions, NAACP, the assassination of President McKinley by an anarchist, the rise of communism, and the suffragette movement endeavoring to grant women the right to vote, even equal standing under United States law, all created deep concern among conservative Christian Churches. Church leaders recoiled from these rapid social changes and challenges – and from appointing women to the position of servant. Even today, this concern is often expressed as a compromise toward, or complete agreement with, egalitarianism – which it is not. William D. Mounce commented, "Whatever the specific interpretation of this verse [1 Tim. 3:11] may be, it is not related to the issue of women in leadership since the deacon(ess) does not provide authoritative leadership. There is no question that women were to play a significant role in serving the church."[35]

"They would have a vote on the Church Board!" As will be demonstrated in a later chapter of this book (Chapter 6), the Church Board – wherein elders and deacons have equal voice and vote on a Board as stipulated in by-laws – was a 20th century

---

[34] Philip Y. Pendleton, *Commentary on Thessalonians, Corinthians, Galatians, and Romans* (Cincinnati: Standard Publishing, 1916), 545.

[35] William D. Mounce, *Word Biblical Commentary, Volume 46: Pastoral Epistles* (Nashville: Thomas Nelson Publishers, 2000), 202.

development in the Restoration Movement. Women had "deaconed" well in these churches for generations; with the advent of new leadership structures and the prospect of women having votes alongside elders and other leaders (while they still couldn't cast votes politically), the conclusion became self-evident in the thinking of many: *we can't have women deacons.* If this sounds like a stretch, consider that in 1927, *Christian Standard* replied to this question: "Do we have any Scripture authority for calling women to the official board to act as deacons?"[36] More recently, a 1990 *Standard* editorial observed, "The problem, it seems to me, is not with what the Scripture says, but with our twentieth-century concept of a 'church board,' and the mind-set that sees in the word 'deaconess' some sort of authority or power."[37] Indeed. In order to preserve an unbiblical approach to church governance, "the board," we removed from our practice the perfectly biblical role of servants – deacons – who are women.

"We've never had women deacons before!" If by "we" one means the Restoration Movement or conservative, Bible-believing traditions, that simply is not true. If by "we" it refers to one's own congregation, then the leadership should explore the church's history to determine if such was always the case. If by "we" it refers to one's personal memory and experience, then it might be true. In the end, the presence of women servants falls to each individual congregation to explore Scripture and decide accordingly.

---

[36] J. B. Briney, "Several Questions Considered," *Christian Standard* (April 2, 1927), 318.

[37] Editor, "Should We Have Deaconesses?" *Christian Standard* (February 18, 1990): 3.

Anecdotally, my wife's home congregation in Memphis, Missouri was founded in 1850, making it among the oldest active Christian Churches / Churches of Christ congregations. While they do not have women servants today, the church records make frequent reference to all of the ministry accomplished by "deaconesses."

Who do you think are the *guna* in 1 Timothy 3:11, and does this understanding affect how you view Phoebe in Romans 16?

Whatever your understanding of *guna*, how does it influence your understanding of "deacon" both biblically and practically?

If your church does not currently have women lead servants, and this chapter has modified your understanding, will you make any changes in your congregation? Why or why not?

If your congregation does not currently have women lead servants, and you want to make changes, create a policy to firmly establish expectations, boundaries, etc. What should it contain? When will it be implemented? How will it be introduced and explained to the congregation and by whom?

Part 2: Historical Perspective

Chapter 4: Deacons in the Restoration Movement

Jim Estep

Consistency

This is not a word one would use to describe the Restoration Movement's understanding of the role and function of the servant/deacon. While virtually all agreed that deacons were primarily servants and were accountable to the elder team, the specifics beyond these generalities varied greatly. For example, the role of the servant in our early history was highly influenced by the denominational roots of our early leaders. Such men as Alexander Campbell and Barton Stone placed emphasis on the elders' leadership, drawn from their Presbyterian heritage; however, the Baptist backgrounds of many comprising the membership of our churches placed great emphasis and value on the ministry of servants.[38]

Alexander Campbell on Servants

The first significant attention was given to servants by Campbell in his *Christian Baptist* article, "A Restoration of the Ancient Order of Things, No. XIX. The Deacon's Office" in 1826. He wrote on the "Deacon's Office" in 1835, echoing his earlier sentiments from the *Christian Baptist*, describing deacons as servants, treasurers, waiting the tables of the congregation, and addressing "all matters of temporal concern," which would

[38] J. Stephen Sandifer, "Deacons, Diaconate," *The Encyclopedia of the Stone-Campbell Movement* (Grand Rapids: Eerdmans Publishing House, 2004), 260.

require a "plurality of deacons in every church" since "the duties are too oppressive for a single individual."[39]

Campbell asserted the need to have a plurality of both elders and servants; those "presiding" – instruction and directing vs. those "ministering," i.e. Overseers and Servants. These are two distinct roles and functions within the congregation; "two distinct offices in reference to its usefulness and happiness – the office of presiding, i.e. instructing and directing; and the office of ministering, i.e. of executing all the wishes of the community … bishops and deacons, or overseers and ministers."[40] As Campbell would explain later, "In the same church there were Deacons, evidently of an inferior order and subsequent appointment, since they are not named in the Acts in connection with the church of Ephesus, and when subsequently mentioned in the letter to Timothy, are always named after the Elders or Bishops."[41]

Campbell opens his piece with an abrupt statement, "The time once was that every christian [sic] congregation had a treasury. In those days they required a steward, a treasurer or a deacon, or more than one, as the exigencies demanded."[42] He proceeds to note that the word deacon simply means servant, but that this is far too generic a treatment of the deacon's office, noting that all Christian leaders regardless of title or position should be a servant; but that deacons were specifically to be "the servants of

---

[39] Alexander Campbell, "Deacon's Office," *Millennial Harbinger* (October 1835, Extra): 507.

[40] Campbell, *Millennial Harbinger* (June 1835): 243.

[41] A ____n, "Nature of the Christian Organization, No. XIII," *Millennial Harbinger* (March 1843): 134.

[42] Alexander Campbell, "A Restoration of the Ancient Order of Things. No. XIX. The Deacon's Office," *Christian Baptist*, 1826 (reprinted 1983), 335.

the church in its temporal concerns. These were the deacons, or stewards, or treasurers of the church."[43]

He then proceeded to outline the various functions of deacons, especially those requiring access to funds, with such diverse functions and significant ministry needs that "a plurality of deacons was in most instances necessary because of the attention required from them and the trust reposed in them," later citing Acts 6 as an example,[43] describing their duties as serving at "the Lord's table, the bishop's table, and the poor's table."[43]

Deacons were in a position so as to be aware of the circumstances of individuals and families within the congregation, and hence able to minister to them. They were tasked with benevolence toward the poor and the widow, as well as caring for the sick, afflicted, and those who were under duress; all funded by the church's treasury.[44] So tied to the treasury was this office in Campbell's thoughts that he critiqued the role of deacon in his own day, "how has it degenerated in modern times into a frivolous and unmeaning carrying about a place once a quarter, in all the meagre pomp of a vane world! – a mere pompous etiquette, without use or meaning."[43]

One final note: Campbell points out that "Amongst the Greeks who paid so much regard to differences of sex, female deacons, or deaconesses, were appointed to visit and wait upon the sisters," noting "Phebe [sic] of Cenchrea, and other persons mentioned in the New Testament, who labored in the gospel."[45] Campbell affirmed the idea of women as lead servants, though he preferred the term "deaconess."

---

[43] Campbell, *The Christian Baptist*, 335.
[44] Campbell, *The Christian Baptist*, 335, 336.

Robert Milligan on Deacons

Following Campbell's treatment of the lead servant in the *Christian Baptist* in the 1830s and 40s, the next most significant attention given to them was in 1855 by Robert Milligan of Bethany College in "The Permanent Orders of the Christian Ministry," which was published as a three-part article in the *Millennial Harbinger*; deacons, elders, and evangelists. In fact, Alexander Campbell himself even provided a paragraph of endorsement for Milligan's work.

Milligan identified the seven mentioned in Acts 6 as deacons, although this should not be taken as a self-evident, foregone conclusion.[45] "The duty of these men was to attend to the secular interests of the congregation," e.g. "those who feed the widows, must have the control of the treasury of the congregation."[46] Following a brief treatment on the qualifications for deacons, laid out in Acts 6, he explains that upon the God-given criteria for qualifying to serve, "the disciples made their election according to this divinely constituted standard. And the apostles expressed their concurrence by solemnly ordaining them to the work for which they had been chosen,"[47] proceeding, then, to spend several pages explaining the nature of ordination, even separately from the subject of deacons.

---

[45] Editorial note: please remember Dr. Roadcup's explanation in the opening chapter that the personal noun form, *diakonos*, is not used of "the seven" chosen in Acts 6. Additionally, they are referenced in Acts 21:8 as "the seven," not as "deacons." Luke never wrote *diakonos* in either his Gospel or Acts, while he used *diakonia*, "the ministry of," once in his Gospel and eight times in Acts.
[46] Robert Milligan, "The Permanent Orders of the Christian Ministry," *Millennial Harbinger* (1855): 625, 626.
[47] Milligan, 627.

Milligan then returns to the subject of deacons, noting "that the seven were all officially equal," i.e. no hierarchy of deacons, no more authority given one than another; just "harmony" so as to "discharge their official duties."[48]

Once again, of note, Milligan too affirmed the value of women deacons. "The Phebes [sic] [i.e., women deacons] should, therefore, constitute a part of the διακονοι [deacons] of every fully organized Christian congregation," which included ministering to "the feeble, the sick, the poor, and the destitute, especially of their own sex."[49]

A Deacon Snapshot from the Mid-19th Century

Perhaps the most definitive job description for deacons was provided in an article by James Challen in 1866, which offered:[50]

1. *He should give special regard to all the secular affairs of the congregation.*
2. *He should attend to the gathering of all the money necessary for the support of the cause and the wants of the poor.*
3. *He should watch over the education of the poor; and be an efficient help in the Sunday school.*
4. *The deacons of the church and the Elders should have their stated meetings for conference and mutual help.*
5. *They should serve at the Table of the Lord.*
6. *They should be earnestly engaged in the cause of Christ, as they stand in the light of representative men of the congregation.*

---

48 Milligan, 633.

49 Milligan, 626.

50 James Challen, "Deacon's Office," *Millennial Harbinger* (Feb. 1866): 56-58.

> 7. *They should see that all debts due by the congregation, should be faithfully paid; and that all repairs for the meeting-house should be made: That fuel should be provided, the house kept in good order, and every comfort compatible with the necessities oft [t]he case be given to the worshipers.*
> 8. *They should call to their aid at stated times others, in the same church, male and female, as occasion requires, that nothing be wanting.*
> 9. *They should be elected for life or during good behavior – The yearly election of elders and deacons is an abomination. It is simply ridiculous and insupportable. Permanency is attached to these offices.*

As one reads through this description of servants from 1866, one can see how they were meeting the contemporary needs of the church, e.g. their service to the Sunday School, while also rejecting the newer idea of annual elections of elders and deacons.

Issues with Deacons

In the decades following the death of our first-generation leaders (Stone, Campbell, Pendleton, Milligan, etc.), the understanding of deacons in almost every aspect came under scrutiny and challenge. J. Steven Sandifer expressed it this way:

> *The exact role of male deacons in the Restoration Movement underwent an evolution. Their activities move from being financial custodians, to varied servants, to ministry system leaders. ... The questions of the early twentieth century concerned interpretations of the qualifications, the meaning of*

> *appointment or ordination, and the role of females. ... The teachings of the mid twentieth century reflected a power struggle between the elders and deacons for control of the congregation and its money.*[51]

What specifically came under review? What shifts in the lead servant's place, function and role occurred in the late 19th to early 20th centuries? The authority of the servant was an issue, since initially it was a servant's position with specified boundaries.[52] For some, lead servants were not to teach or preach, such as Milligan's opinion that they could not teach as an officer of the church;[53] others, in contrast, later asserted that servants needed to both preach and teach. Tolbert Fanning reassessed the notion of "deacon" being more a descriptive term than position or office in the church. Others raised issue with how individuals became deacons – was it by elder appointment or congregational vote? Interrelated amongst all of this was the question of whether servants were to receive ordination, and if so, by whom, especially in the absence of Apostles (keeping in mind the subtle ambiguities presented by Acts 6).[54] Early Restoration Movement leaders almost universally affirmed that the seven of Acts 6 were indeed the first "deacons," but now even this notion came under question. That confusion, in turn, raised the practical quandary

---

[51] J. Stephen Sandifer, *Deacons: Male and Female* (Self Published, 1989), 119, 144.
[52] Sandifer, 261.
[53] Milligan, 626.
[54] Compare Alexander Campbell, "Queries," *Millennial Harbinger* (Mar 1855): 173; William K. Pendleton, "Ordination of Elders and Deacons," *Millennial Harbinger* (September 1865): 423.

of how the qualifications of servants were to be interpreted and applied.[55]

Confusion over the office of deacon in the mid-1800s was exemplified by an exchange of letters between one of our most notable leaders, William K. Pendleton, with one John C. Miller of Nineveh, IN, in two pieces published in the *Millennial Harbinger* in 1870 entitled "The Deacon's Office" and "The Deacon's Office Again."[56] Similarly, in *Gospel Advocate*, J. Roy Vaughan described the struggle for power in the church between elders and deacons. He rejected the notion of elders over the spiritual and deacons over the physical, instead affirming the authority of elders over everything with servants being a task force, accomplishing the ministry of the church.[57]

As detailed in the previous chapter, another major issue was the legitimacy of women in the role of lead servant. "Virtually all Stone-Campbell writers of the nineteenth century advocated female deacons in the churches, though most were clear to distinguish deaconesses' ministry from that of deacons," being primarily work with other women and/or children.[59] It was not until 1906 that J. W. McGarvey opposed the role of the deaconess altogether, failing to recognize women as deacons. Many northern churches retained female deacons while southern churches did not. [58]

Sandifer refers to 20th Century shifts in congregational leadership, and how it influenced the role of elder and deacon, as the *military*

---

[55] Thomas Campbell, "Queries by A.S.H.," *Millennial Harbinger* (May 1845): 220

[56] *Millennial Harbinger* (March 1870): 136-146; *Millennial Harbinger* (May 1870): 250-258.

[57] J. Roy Vaughan, "The Deacons," *Gospel Advocate* (September 20, 1951): 594.

[58] Sandifer, *Encyclopedia of the SCM*, 261.

and *team* approaches. In the military model, the officers (elders) retained much of the authority within the congregation with the enlisted (deacons) carrying out their orders and performing assigned tasks. Later, the team approach called for elders and deacons to be considered virtually equal with simply different functions and areas of ministry rather than the previous hierarchical structure.[59]

As the Restoration Movement enters its second century of existence, similar questions and challenges remain. Some churches have dropped the title "deacon" completely and replaced it with "ministry team leader," "lead servant," or perhaps the most descriptive term, "servant leader." Changes in terminology have also been a means of reintroducing women into the role and function of servant. In other congregations, the shifting roles of governance have made the staff "elders," and the elders "deacons," eliminating the recognized presence of deacons/servants altogether.

Simply put, deacons lead through serving, caring for others, doing ministry to those who Jesus called "the least of these," and sharing the love of Christ throughout the church and community in which it ministers.

---

[59] Sandifer, *Encyclopedia of the SCM*, 260.

How would you summarize the early Restoration Movement's understanding of servants?

With all the issues listed in the mid-19th century and early 20th century, where do you land on matters of servant authority, role, function, and relation to the elders?

How are servants ("deacons") described in your current congregation? How does this compare to the historic record of our Movement's churches?

Chapter 5: Deacons & Elder Governance

Gary Johnson

"All hands on deck!"

For centuries, this command has been heard aboard ships of all shapes and sizes in all manner of languages. When necessary, a ship's captain would issue this order with urgency, as each sailor was needed immediately at their respective posts. Though this phrase has nautical roots, its essence is rooted in the early days of the first century Church. There came a time when the Apostles gave the proverbial command: "all hands on deck," and it was in this moment that the role of deacon was created.

At the time, the first century Church was experiencing significant growing pains. Prior to the Great Persecution of Acts 7-8, the Jerusalem congregation grew by leaps and bounds. In Acts 4:4, we read that "the number of men grew to about five thousand," meaning that when women and children were added to the head count, the church could have easily numbered twenty thousand or more. This rapid growth brought with it all manner of challenges, one of which is described in Acts 6:1-7.

> *In those days when the number of disciples was increasing, the Hellenistic Jews among them complained against the Hebraic Jews because their widows were being overlooked in the daily distribution of food. So the Twelve gathered all the disciples together and said, "It would not be right for us to neglect the ministry of the word of God in order to wait on tables. Brothers and sisters, choose seven men from among you who are known to be full of the Spirit and wisdom. We will turn this*

responsibility over to them and will give our attention to prayer and the ministry of the word." This proposal pleased the whole group. They chose Stephen, a man full of faith and of the Holy Spirit; also Philip, Procorus, Nicanor, Timon, Parmenas, and Nicolas from Antioch, a convert to Judaism. They presented these men to the apostles, who prayed and laid their hands on them. So the word of God spread. The number of disciples in Jerusalem increased rapidly, and a large number of priests became obedient to the faith. (NIV)

Behind the Scenes

To best understand the impact of this text, we must go behind the scenes and understand the context of the event. While numerical growth was rapid and continuous (v. 1), a group of Greek-speaking widows were going hungry. The Greek tense of the word "overlooked" means that the widows went hungry day after day; it was not a one-time occurrence. Moreover, in the first century, people worked to live for just another day – it was a survivalist society. Unlike us, families did not eat three meals a day. To the contrary, individuals ate one meal a day – if that. These widows with Greek roots were living in Jerusalem, far from home, and did not have family to care for them.

Yet, with the Church growing by thousands, the Apostles were no longer able to "wait on tables," a phrase that refers to a time-honored practice among God's people. In Old Testament times, God commanded His people to care for widows, orphans and foreigners. Hence, to "wait on tables" meant that church leaders went door-to-door and collected food for these people in need. Yet, for some reason, the Greek-speaking widows went to bed hungry night after night – until seven men stepped in.

"Known to be full of the Spirit and wisdom," these seven men were spiritually strong and committed. It is important to note that all seven men had Greek names, meaning that these individuals had heartfelt concern for and commitment to their widows. The Apostles prayed over these men and "laid their hands on them," which was quite significant. In this instance, the laying on of hands indicated the giving of authority. In Numbers 27:18-23, God told Moses to have Joshua stand before the people and then lay hands on him, giving Joshua some of the leadership authority of Moses. Similarly, the Apostles gave these seven men not only the responsibility of feeding the widows, but also the authority by which to lead that ministry.

By delegating both responsibility and authority to gifted and capable men, the Apostles were able to devote themselves to "prayer and the ministry of the word." The word "ministry" in verse four is the Greek noun *diakonia* (διακονια) which means "the work of, the service of." It's one of the Greek words from which the English word "deacon" is derived. The Apostles ensured hungry widows were given physical bread, while they, then, provided the believers spiritual bread. With other men serving alongside them, the Apostles concentrated on the priority of spiritually caring for the growing congregation.

Front and Center

How does this moment in the first century speak to this moment in the 21st century church? There is much from behind the scenes that must be front and center for the Church today, and it has much to do with how the local church is structured.

The human body is formed on and around our skeletal system. Our bones not only give us form and function, but their marrow is the primary supplier of the many new blood cells we need daily. Simply put, our overall health depends significantly on our skeletal system. Likewise, the health of the local church is significantly impacted by how the local church is structured and that structure is clearly depicted in the book of Acts. We at e2 call this structure *elder governance*. When we look closely at the function of elders in the early church, it is easy to see that these men focused on five key responsibilities as spiritual leaders: **prayer**, **preaching**, **policy**, **protection** and **pastoral care**.

Again, in Acts 6:1-7, the Apostles offloaded the daily task of feeding widows to a carefully chosen group of men, which enabled them to devote themselves to **prayer** and **preaching**. The Apostles realized that the spiritual health and vitality of the church was their responsibility and they needed time to actually care for those needs in the church. They were not the only people praying, but they fostered an environment in which the believers often prayed. They were both *preaching* the Word (i.e., exhortation), and *teaching* the Word as well (i.e., explanation).

In Acts 15, we read of the Jerusalem Council, a gathering of Apostles and elders to decide on a pressing and recurring question: do Gentiles have to obey the Law of Moses and be circumcised to become Christians? In Acts 11, the church in Jerusalem sent Barnabas to Antioch, where he and Paul brought many people to Christ and discipled them in the faith. This is where "the disciples were called Christians first" (Acts 11:26). Directed by the Holy Spirit to begin their first missionary journey (Acts 13:1-3), Paul and Barnabas left Antioch and later returned, only to discover that other teachers had made their way into that church and instructed people to obey the Law of Moses. The conflict over this issue was so significant that those involved turned to the church leaders in Jerusalem – the Apostles and elders – for them to resolve the conflict. James, the half-brother of Jesus, was known as the chief elder of the Jerusalem congregation. After listening to each perspective on this weighty issue, James declared: “we should not make it difficult for the Gentiles who are turning to God” (v. 19, NIV). A letter was then drafted by the church leaders for Paul, Barnabas, Silas, and Barsabbas to take to Antioch and read to the church, implementing what had been decided by the Apostles and elders. In this instance, a **policy** was developed and on-boarded. Elders establish policy, then give it to staff and others (i.e. servant leaders / deacons) to implement and utilize in the church.

In Acts 20:13-38, Paul gathered the elders of the church of Ephesus at the neighboring town of Miletus (v. 17) so that he could turn in his proverbial letter of resignation. Paul had earlier been in ministry at Ephesus for three years (v. 31), and now in his final farewell to them, Paul commanded them to “Keep watch over yourselves and all the flock of which the Holy Spirit has made you overseers…” (v. 28, NIV). Paul warned them that soon after his departure “savage wolves will come in among you and will not spare the flock” (v. 29, NIV). Elders provide **protection** for the local church. The 21st century church is spiritually under assault. Increasing numbers of congregations and denominations are rejecting orthodox Christian belief, and elders are responsible to protect the beliefs of the church. To do so, elders must study the Word, know the Word, and must both know and embrace sound doctrine. Because this responsibility demands that elders protect the church from all that is spiritually dark, elders oversee church discipline when necessary.

We also see in Acts 20 that Paul called for the elders to provide **pastoral care** to the local church. Paul said, “… Be shepherds of the church of God…” (v. 28, NIV). The word for “shepherds” means to be pastoral. Elders must know and move among the people of the church, helping them spiritually to be at their best. As the flock (i.e., congregation) increases in size, elders are to equip and empower others to help with the pastoral care of people. This can happen through a variety of ministries, such as Celebrate Recovery, Divorce Care, Grief Share, a small groups / life group ministry, and others. Though elders may not be providing for each and every act of pastoral care for each and every believer, they must make certain that a system of care is alive and active in the local church.

When elders lead spiritually and devote themselves to 1) prayer, 2) preaching, 3) policy, 4) protection, and 5) pastoral care, the church becomes healthy … and healthy things grow. Elder governance works. Whether the church is 50 or 5,000 in size, this structure demands that elders function as spiritual leaders, mindful of the condition of the whole church. They pursue and practice these five God-given responsibilities.

Weed Control

Whether getting rid of weeds in a lawn or farm field, weed control is a multi-billion-dollar industry in the United States. We invest time and money trying to have a perfect lawn or crop, and the same effort must be made by elders of the local church to rid themselves of unnecessary weeds. The work of elders is often mired down in the weeds.

The typical structure of the local church lends itself to producing a field of weeds. Most churches in America are small, averaging less than 150 in size. Why? They operate with a church board structure. Once a month, the church board meets. Sitting around the table are elders, deacons, trustees, and the preacher. Besides the preacher, these individuals have been nominated and elected to an office, in which they serve for a stated term (i.e., 2 years, 3 years, etc.). The board follows Roberts Rules of Order. Motions are made, then seconded, discussion happens, and a vote is then taken. Some win and some lose. This structure looks more like the American form of government than the New Testament, yet we wonder aloud why churches are often in conflict. This is one of the many ways in which churches are unhealthy, which results in churches not growing. To become healthy, churches must *repent* of this structure and intentionally pattern themselves after elder governance found in Acts.

To practice weed control, elders must do two things: eliminate and delegate. Eliminate working in the weeds. Elders do not balance the church checking account. They do not develop the annual budget. Elders do not get bids on new HVAC systems or parking lot improvements.

Elders provide pastoral care, know and defend the doctrine of the church, establish and implement policy, and most importantly, feed the flock spiritually. Elders' meeting agendas need five "buckets:" **prayer**, **preaching**, **policy**, **protection** and **pastoral care**. Items that logically fit in one of these five categories get added. If an item doesn't fit, then it belongs on someone else's to-do list (i.e. a staff member, lead servant, etc.).

Elders delegate. Jesus did. He equipped and empowered the seventy, sending them out two-by-two. We must recruit, equip and empower people to serve in the local church, using their spiritual gifts and skills accordingly. In 1 Peter 4:10, we are reminded that every person has received spiritual gifts from the Lord and that we are to use those abilities for the express purpose of advancing the kingdom of God. Moreover, there is a spiritual gift of leadership or administration listed by Paul in Romans 12:8, and if a person has received that gifting, that individual can lead in the area of his or her giftedness. For example, perhaps a person is gifted in mercy and compassion, as well as in leadership. This individual could lead a team of merciful, compassionate volunteers to minister to the emotional needs of people (i.e., those grieving, depressed, anxious, addicted, etc.). Another example may be an individual skilled in working with their hands, and also with the gift of leadership. This individual could lead a group of volunteers caring for the church building and grounds.

These individuals are servants – deacons – of Jesus. The local church needs men and women willing and able to serve the local church in the area of their giftedness and calling. These servants enable elders to get out of the proverbial weeds and pursue their greater responsibilities while servants willingly get into the weeds, providing all manner of help in the day-to-day work of the church. As in Acts 6:6, servants, both men and women, serve at the request and appointment of the elders. Elders must give servants not only jobs to do, but the authority to accomplish their work. Elders are not to micro-manage people, whether they be staff or volunteers in the church. People must be trusted to serve, and to serve well.

An A+ Attitude

This transition to elder governance, with the help of men and women serving, will only happen if a particular attitude is present. An attitude resides in the mind and results in certain behavior. After all, how we think determines how we act.

When writing to the church at Philippi, Paul addressed "overseers and [servants]" (1:1) – the only such time that Paul co-addressed one of his letters not only to a church, but explicitly to her leaders. In his letter, Paul addressed conflict in the church:

"I plead with Euodia and I plead with Syntyche to be of the same mind in the Lord" (4:2, NIV). Earlier, Paul called for the entire congregation to have and show humility with each other (2:1-4). For that to happen, Paul cited the attitude of Jesus as an example worth following.

> *...have the same mindset as Christ Jesus:*
> *Who, being in very nature God,*
> *did not consider equality with God something to*
> *be used to his own advantage;*
> *rather, he made himself nothing*
> *by taking the very nature of a servant,*
> *being made in human likeness.*
> *And being found in appearance as a man,*
> *he humbled himself*
> *by becoming obedient to death—*
> *even death on a cross!*
>
> *Philippians 2:5-8* (NIV)

Jesus did not consider positional authority with God something to hold tightly, but He emptied Himself of that desire. In humility, "the Son of Man did not come to be served, but to serve, and to give His life as a ransom for many" (Mk. 10:45, NIV). In humility, Jesus was born to a peasant girl and her blue-collar carpenter husband. In humility, the newborn Jesus was laid in an animal's feeding trough out in a stable. In humility, Jesus lived His life serving others. His humble attitude is worth emulating if we are to transition to a biblical model of church structure.

Nik Wallenda is known worldwide as a high wire aerialist. In recent years – and thanks to cable television – people around the world viewed him walking across Niagara Falls and the Grand Canyon. Moreover, Wallenda is known by God as a follower of Jesus – and he admits that he is a Christian who struggles with pride. To fight this temptation, Wallenda has developed a personal discipline. After the media and crowds leave an event, Wallenda moves into action. In his book *Balance* (Faith Works, 2013, p. 207), Wallenda writes:

> *My purpose is simply to help clean up after myself. The huge crowd left a great deal of trash behind, and I feel compelled to pitch in. Besides, after the inordinate amount of attention I sought and received, I need to keep myself grounded. Three hours of cleaning up debris is good for my soul. Humility does not come naturally to me. So if I have to force myself into situations that are humbling, so be it .... I know that I need to get down on my hands and knees like everyone else. I do it because it's a way to keep from tripping. As a follower of Jesus, I see him washing the feet of others. I do it because if I don't serve others I'll be serving nothing but my ego.*

Humility means that we move to a lower place. Jesus certainly did so when He left His royal position in Heaven and came to earth to die for us on a cross. For elders to practice "weed control," they must humble themselves and intentionally do the work of elders, while delegating responsibility and authority to men and women to serve the local church in keeping with their spiritual gifts and skills. When that happens, the local church becomes healthy – and healthy things grow.

Describe the current structure of your church's leadership?

How is the current structure different than elder governance as described in the chapter?

What obstacles may hinder your congregation's shift to elder governance?

What are the first steps you could take toward moving to elder governance?

Chapter 6: Deacons & the Church Board

Jim Estep

"Flintstones! Meet the Flintstones ..."

The best part of the cartoon, and even the movies, was how they adapted modern technology and appliance concepts into a Stone Age context. Pterodactyls were airplanes, running water in homes came from elephants' trunks, small dinosaurs were lawnmowers, and large sauropods were cranes or other construction equipment. It was creative – but fake. They showed the full creative imagination of people depicting 20th-21st century AD daily life in a Stone Age context. But life in the Stone Age was indeed different. To put the Flintstones in theological terms, it is eisegesis; that is, putting a meaning into a context that cannot accommodate it. Eisegesis is the interpreting of a biblical text in the current reader's context rather than the original one. Rather than letting the text speak for itself, we impose meanings and structures into/onto the text.[60]

To a certain extent this is inevitable. The dynamics of church governance, its structure and function, are often influenced by the culture in which the church exists. One can see the similarities of the Roman Catholic Church's multi-tiered hierarchical structure to that of the Roman Empire. Similarly, the churches of the Reformation formed synods and other administrative structures common to their own national cultures of the time. The Restoration Movement has never been immune

---

[60] Much of this chapter was originally published by me as "Thus Saith the Board" in *Christian Standard* (February 23, 1992): 6-8.

to such influences. Our historical context has, to a degree, shaped our approach to the biblical text.

For example, one of our founding voices, Alexander Campbell, compared our church governance to that of the fledgling United States' governmental structure.

> *Our, and all political governments in civilized countries, have three departments – the legislative, the judicial, and the executive. In the Christian community Jesus is lawgiver and judge – his apostles announce his laws and statutes – and the executive part of all that belongs to the ordinary communities, built upon the foundation, not of bishops and deacons, but of apostles and prophets – Jesus himself the chief cornerstone.*[61]

The Restoration Movement has always sought to adhere to the pattern of the New Testament, especially to restore New Testament church governance. But have we, in fact, actually restored the structure and organization in the church in accordance with New Testament teachings? Have we allowed cultural influences to distract us from the biblical text?

While one may frequently hear the phrase "elders and deacons" in the vernacular of the Christian Churches / Churches of Christ today, amazingly, it occurs only once in the New Testament (Phil. 1:1, "overseers and deacons"). Yet, in the vast majority of our congregations the church is governed by a church board or "joint board," usually consisting of elders and deacons who make decisions together, with equal voting authority in all matters.

---

[61] Alexander Campbell, "To Dr. James H. Otey, Bishop of Tennessee, Letter II," *Millennial Harbinger* (June 1835): 243.

The board as a whole can overrule a decision made by the elders alone by simply outnumbering the elders in a board vote; hence the joint board is the authority in the church, and non-elders have more leadership than the elders.

Where does the concept of a joint board come from? Is it from the New Testament? Did Campbell, Stone, or other early Restoration Movement pioneers originate this form of church polity? When did the joint board come into our movement?

New Testament and Church Boards?

The concept of a joint church board of elders and deacons through which all church decisions are made or ratified is irreconcilable with several New Testament principles and precedents. First, it is obvious that the responsibility for oversight in the early church was given to the elders or overseers (Acts 11:30, 14:23, 15:2, 20:17; 1 Tim. 5:17; 1 Pet. 5:1-4). While this does not diminish the value of servants, it does indicate that servants are not those appointed to lead the congregation.

Second, in several instances in the New Testament, servants are absent from the discussion of the leadership structures or even from the ministry of the church, thus prohibiting the idea of a joint board. For example, in the entirety of both the books of Acts and Titus, elders are depicted, described, and we see them in action, but servants are never mentioned.[62]

---

[62] Many equate deacons with the men chosen in Acts 6; however, the term διακονος/deacon is never used to describe the men directly. Their action is depicted via the verb form (v. 2), and the ministry role with the noun form (v. 1; διακονια), but the personal noun *diakonos* is never used directly of the men.

Third, the English word *deacon* is taken from the Greek word διακονος (diakonos), which means "servant." The terms elder and overseer, *presbuteros* and *episkopos*, respectively, denote the Jewish term for leader (elder) and the Greek term for leader (overseer). In the New Testament, the title of servant is obviously reserved to those who are given the responsibility of serving within the church. Those given responsibility of overseeing or who "rule well" are given the label "elder."

The idea of a joint board is foreign to the history and letters of the New Testament. It is, quite simply, the product of cultural eisegesis.

Early Restoration Leaders and the Absence of Church Boards

The idea of a joint board was also foreign to the early leaders of the Restoration Movement. The early leaders of our movement were prolific writers. The issues and debates that affected the development of our movement in its infancy are reflected in the articles and periodicals of the editors Barton W. Stone (*Christian Messenger*) and Alexander Campbell (*Christian Baptist* and *Millennial Harbinger*). The content of these periodicals reflects the beliefs and attitudes of the early leaders of the Restoration Movement.

What did those men say about the biblical teaching on church organization? In not one article on the subject of church structure, organization, or government, is any mention given to the concept of a joint board. Nor are deacons suggested to have equal authority with the elders in the congregation. While the titles "board of deacons" and "board of elders" may have been sparingly employed, these were two separate entities, and their respective roles were never confused.

In fact, oftentimes the writers seemed to neglect or minimize the function of servants, while emphasizing the responsibility and authority of the elders. One could read articles written about elders in the absence of any discussion of deacons; however, one is hard pressed to locate a treatment of deacons without elders being introduced into the dialog. Why might that be the case? It is because elders can lead in contexts and matters unrelated to the work of servants, but the servants of the church need elders for guidance and direction.

It was the position of Alexander Campbell (1788-1866) that the elders retained the responsibility for oversight of the congregation. He wrote three prominent articles on elders but only one regarding deacons. In these he stridently emphasized the oversight function of the elders, with no mention of deacons having any part in their decision making or execution of duties.[63]

In his writing on church government, Campbell rarely included the office of deacon, since he considered it "of an inferior order and subsequent appointment ... [and] always named after the Elders or Bishops."[64] As one may notice, Campbell's attitude toward servants, by today's impression, is almost insulting and degrading. However, when Campbell wrote these articles, the work of the deacon was never equated with that of the elder and was seen as that of an appointed servant to fulfill a particular task. There was no joint board concept in the congregation. Thus, the "office" of deacon was just as he described – i.e. an "office" of service.

---

[63] Compare Alexander Campbell, *The Christian Baptist* (March 1826): 231-233, 242-243; (4, 1827): 260-261.

[64] Alexander Campbell, *Millennial Harbinger* (March 1843): 134.

Alongside Alexander Campbell in the early Restoration Movement, Barton W. Stone (1772-1844) was, similarly, a highly influential and guiding voice. His *Christian Messenger* did not focus on the topic of church government to the degree of Campbell's periodicals, but it did parallel the thoughts and ideas of Campbell on the subject of elders' and servants' roles. In fact, while Campbell and Stone differed on the relationship and role of the Evangelist/Pastor and the Bishops/Elders,[65] they did not differ on the role of servants as the appointed and recognized ones who carried out the ministries of the church. In short, Stone and Campbell shared a common perception on the authority of the elders, and servanthood of the deacons.

To further illustrate the point, in 1855, Robert Milligan penned three seminal articles for the *Millennial Harbinger*. The series of articles, entitled "The Permanent Orders of the Christian Ministry," addressed the function and role of deacons, elders, and evangelists. When describing them, not only is the absence of a joint board readily apparent, but the affirmation of the separation of these "Orders" is quite intentional.

It is apparent that the practice of a joint church board of elders and deacons in the Christian Churches / Churches of Christ did not originate in the mind of Campbell or Stone, nor any of the early contributors to their journals. The periodical literature of the early Restoration Movement offers no indication of the existence of a joint board composed of elders and deacons being in existence up through the death of Campbell in 1866.

---

[65] For a more detailed discussion of this disagreement, see Chapter 4 "We Vs. Them Mentality" of our earlier work *Conflict|Resolution,* pp. 51-54.

Church Boards later in the Movement

Where did the joint board come from? Once again, the periodicals allow us to trace the development of the joint board concept from 1866 to the present. Just prior to the death of Campbell the phrase "elders and deacons" became more common, even though it was only used once in the New Testament and rarely by the early leaders in the movement.

While insignificant in its own right, in 1865, the *Millennial Harbinger* published two articles suggesting that the church should form "a board of deacons or elders ... in harmony with the duties of their office, and transact their own official business."[66] This represents the first use of the phrase "board of deacons or elders" in any Restoration periodical. Soon thereafter, another author remarked that "the deacons of the church and the Elders should have their stated meeting for conference and mutual help."[67] In these two articles, one may well witness the incipient concept of a joint church board.

When was the first actual mentioning of the "church board?" Roughly one generation after the articles just mentioned, the *Christian Standard* published an anonymous editorial written by "Sigma" in which the author debated who should have the authority in the church. The title of the article was "Eldership, Presbytery, or Church Board, or Elders and Deacons."[68] It is obvious by the title that the author understands the authority of the church to lie either within the elders/presbytery or the

---

[66] D. P. Henderson, A. S. Shotwell and James Trabue, *Millennial Harbinger* (December, 1865): 673.
[67] James Challen, *Millennial Harbinger* (February, 1866): 57.
[68] Sigma, "Eldership, Presbytery, or Church Board, or Elders and Deacons," *Christian Standard* (February 9, 1895): 132.

church board/elders and deacons. The debate over church governance structure was beginning.

The article proceeds to outline the various problems created by this new form of church government in regard to authority, even mentioning the introduction of "trustees" into the Christian Churches/Churches of Christ.[69] Why trustees? It was because of a shift in the role of the deacon and the advent of by-laws. While only fragmented material is offered in the periodicals between 1866 and 1985 as to the origin of the joint church board, it is quite evident that it occurred because of a change of attitude concerning the role of servants in the church. In his monumental study, *Deacons: Male and Female? A Study for Churches of Christ*, J. Stephen Sandifer explains that both within and outside the Restoration Movement the role of deacons began to shift to "more of an administrative, business, and management role to the neglect of the caring and supportive ministries."[70] In 1883 a series of anonymous editorials were published under the name of "M," who adamantly argued that the function of deacon was far more reaching than previously discussed, stating that it even included teaching and preaching, which historically had been reserved for the elders.[71]

It was this article, anonymously written, that began a fierce exchange of ideas concerning the nature of deacons that would extend into the 20th century. In 1884, two more anonymous articles appeared in the *Christian Standard*, both advocating the

[69] *Christian Standard* (February 9, 1895): 12.
[70] J. Stephen Sandifer, *Deacons* (Self Published, 1989), 112; see pp. 126-143 for in-depth citations from across the Restoration Movement in this regard.
[71] "M," *Christian Standard* (May 12, 1883): 220.

elevating of the role and authority of deacons, arguing for equal office with the elders, but with divided responsibilities.[72]

The trend to elevate the authority of "servants" continued until, by the turn of the century, the church board had come into its contemporary form, and was an accepted practice among our churches. R. H. Bolton wrote in 1901, "The officers of elders and deacons, the elders assuming charge of the spiritual interests of the congregation, while the deacons assume charge of the temporal affairs thereof."[73] In fact, by 1916, conferences were already being held as to how to have an efficient church board structure in the local church.[74]

These ideas continued well into the 20th century, becoming the accepted practice of churches within the Restoration Movement. For example, R. C. Hasting devoted an entire chapter to the work of "The Joint Board," which noted that the responsibilities of elders and deacons are indeed distinct, that out of necessity in smaller and larger churches they work jointly, in the spirit of 2 Corinthians 6:1 "workers together with him," including the election of a Chairman and other appointees typical to an American business model.[75]

While in the early writings of the Restoration Movement the board of elders and board of deacons were mentioned as two separate entities, at the turn of the 20th century, they seem to be

---

[72] *Christian Standard* (November 15, 1884): 362; (November 22, 1884): 370.
[73] R. H. Bolton, *Christian Standard* (May 25, 1901): 652; cf. A. C. VanDyke, *Christian Standard* (April 2, 1900): 448.
[74] J. H. Jones, *Christian Standard* (January 1, 1916): 429.
[75] R. C. Harding, *Handbook for Elders and Deacons* (Cincinnati: Standard Publishing, 1932), 107-119.

combined into a Church Board or "Joint Board," which became common.

The Church had been incorporated.

How the Church Board Developed

We have answered *when* the joint board entered the congregations of the Christian Churches / Churches of Christ, but we have not addressed *why*. Why in the closing years of the 19th century did the joint board appear in our churches? Why not sooner? The answer is historically obvious.

The Church has always reflected its surrounding culture. For example, the images of the leader in the New Testament are drawn from the Jewish background (e.g. elder) and the rural/agricultural setting (e.g. shepherd) in which it was written.

In latter centuries, the church employed terminology from its culture to define and identify aspects of its function and ministry. In the late 19th century, the business climate had a profound effect on our churches. The post-Civil War economy made drastic changes toward industrialization. With the arrival of the Industrial Age also came the rise of "Corporate America."

It was from the corporate structure of American business that the church adopted a new and innovative understanding of congregational polity – the church board. For example, W. L. Hayden wrote in 1984 that "the same business principles which experience has attested in successful enterprise of worldly affairs should be applied in Christian work. These require regular meetings of this board of ecclesiastical financiers."[76]

The church literally incorporated itself, not just in name (as required by law) but in actual, day-to-day practices. Many churches even had their own corporate seal! This led to the inevitable "drawing up of bylaws for a local church of Christ."[77] In the beginning of the Restoration Movement, no church board existed because no corporate boards existed in the United States. Hence, no such concept could have influenced the writings of Campbell and Stone on the issue of church polity. It was not until 1866, after Campbell's death, that the incipient forms of the church board began to appear in the periodical literature of our movement.

The rise of corporate structure in the 1870s parallels the exact time in which our churches began to change from a "presbytery," identifying the elders as possessing the authority, toward a "joint board" form of polity, wherein authority is shared between voting elders and deacons. By the arrival of the 20th century, the joint board was almost universally accepted and practiced among the congregations of our brotherhood.

Board-Certified or God-ordained?

While the Flintstones are comical and entertaining, a Stone Age parody of today, they were not meant to depict the reality of life in prehistoric times. When we do similarly with Scripture – force

---

[76] W. L. Hayden, *Church Polity* (Chicago: S. J. Clarke, 1894), 67. Cf. also L. R. Wilson, Congregational Development (Nashville: Gospel Advocate Company, 1977), 53-58.
[77] G. M. Elliot, *Elder's-Deacon's Manual* (Cincinnati: Christian Restoration Society, 1968), 38.

modern contrivances of leadership and administration into the church in direct contradiction to God's design expressed in Scripture – it is *not* comical. Far too often, it is fatal.

The church board did not originate with Paul or any other New Testament writer. Likewise, it was not formulated by Campbell, Stone, or any other early voice in the early Restoration Movement. Rather, it was a later development in our brotherhood, stimulated by the influence of American corporate structures in the late 19th century.

The question remaining, then, is this: should we govern the church based on our own form of business organization, or on the principles contained in God's Word?

Are we God's people or just stockholders?

How would you describe the general design of your congregation's governance? Is it a board?

What is the relationship of elders and deacons on the organizational chart?

How are the roles of elders and deacons distinguished from one another? Differentiated?

In light of the chapter, what is your reaction or application of it to your congregation or ministry?

Part 3: Relational Considerations

Chapter 7: Deacons & Elders at their Best

Gary Johnson

Some stories are legend, such as the one from a Florida courtroom when a judge and attorney settled an argument between the two of them with a brawl out back. Courtroom video and its accompanying audio depicts escalating tension between the presiding judge, John Murphy, and the attorney for the defendant, Andrew Weinstock. The video also reveals the judge inviting the attorney to a hallway behind the courtroom, and though not on camera, the ensuing fight was stopped by two deputies. The judge was placed on leave and all his cases were reassigned while he sought counseling for anger management.[78]

Conflict is not limited to courtrooms. It is also often be found in congregations, and at times, between elders and deacons. Stories are myriad and legend about deacons out-voting elders at the monthly church board meeting and of elders working to keep certain deacons from being "promoted" to elder in the church. Significant tension can exist between elders and deacons, and rather than resolve the conflict biblically, people are content to allow strained relationships to remain, worsen, and even boil over into outright animosity.

---

[78]https://web.archive.org/web/20140608093758/https://www.latimes.com/nation/nationnow/la-na-nn-florida-judge-lawyer-hallway-fight-20140603-story.html accessed Feb 11, 2020

Why Elders and Deacons Strive Against Each Other: A-B-C

Before exploring how elders and deacons can thrive relationally with one another, we must first understand why we struggle and strive against each other, and it's as simple as A-B-C.

A for Attitude: Human nature thinks first and foremost about self. Our culture is rooted in "me, myself and I" thinking, and with the passing of time, those roots only grow deeper. Consider the following progression in print media. In 1936, LIFE magazine came on the scene, and it was joined decades later in 1974 by *People* magazine. Then, in a short three years, we began seeing *US Weekly* on the newsstand. Only two years later, the magazine *Self* joined the fray. From "life" to "people" to "us" to "self;" how long will it be before we begin reading a magazine that is all about ME?

The spotlight of our minds (i.e., our attitudes) are focused on ourselves. When that happens, we think little about those around us, particularly about those who are in working relationships within the church. Elders and deacons with selfish attitudes have broken relationships. They will not be at their best with one another.

B for Behavior: How we think (i.e., attitudes) determines our behavior. A simple test to see if we struggle with me-minded attitudes is to take note of our behavior. We must ask these four questions of ourselves:

1) Do we have to be in the fastest lane of traffic or the shortest check-out line in a store?
2) Are we quick to criticize others while trying to build ourselves up?

3) Do we frequently use the pronouns "me, myself, I" in conversation with others?
4) Are we easily offended when not recognized or acknowledged?

If we honestly respond to these four questions, we can determine from our behavior the depth of our "me-minded" thinking. Again, it is easy to see in our culture the prevalence of human pride and self-exultation. Consider Hollywood and its award shows. The first Academy Awards (i.e., Oscars) took place in 1927, and since that time, more award shows have followed: the Emmys, Golden Globes, Grammys, People's Choice, Critic's Choice, Screen Actors Guild, Producers Guild, Writers Guild, Directors Guild, MTV Movie, and more. These are just some of the 564 award shows today (1.5 per day), awarding 4,025 trophies (1 every 2 hours). Hollywood sure enjoys being in the spotlight.

In a word, it's pride; a cancer that has metastasized throughout our culture, coast-to-coast, home-to-home, person-to-person. And God hates it. Why? Ego leaves no room for Him. Think of E.G.O. as "edging God out." We edge God out of our lives, thinking that we have made it in life in our strength and with our talent. We are of the opinion that we have amassed all that we have and polished the talent and skills we possess in our strength. We "edge God out" with our over-active ego, so it should not surprise us that James 4:6 states: "God opposes the proud but gives grace to the humble."

Me-minded attitudes result in prideful behaviors that damage relationships between elders and deacons. Power is rooted in pride, and power struggles between leaders in the church can create significant disunity.

C for Communication: Words wound people. The more careless the words, the deeper the wound. When we speak before we think, we reap what we sow. Jesus said that out of the abundance of the heart, an individual speaks; meaning that whatever a person thinks, he speaks. Whether verbally with words or virtually on social media platforms, people express themselves – whether with helpful or hurtful words.

There are five types of conversation that deepen with each level:

1. Cliché – shallow, even meaningless talk between people
2. Facts – sharing indisputable information (i.e., "The sun is bright today.")
3. Opinion – sharing our personal views about issues, opening ourselves to rejection
4. Feeling – sharing emotions
5. Honesty – completely candid, transparent conversation, saying the proverbial last 10%

Because people do not want to be rejected by others, they seldom express opinions or feelings with one another. When conversation remains shallow and only fact-filled, relationships cannot be at their best. Similarly, elders and deacons struggle relationally because they do not choose to intentionally communicate with one another at deeper, more significant levels than clichés and facts.

How Elders and Deacons Can Thrive

As brothers in Christ, elders and deacons can thrive with one another relationally, particularly when they follow the teaching and example of Jesus. In Luke 9, Jesus knew that the time for Him to ascend to heaven was fast approaching (verse 51). To ascend, He had first to die on a cross, be buried in a tomb and be raised from the dead. Hence, Luke 9 is the beginning of the end of His life, and in His final days with His followers, Jesus called something out.

> *An argument started among the disciples as to which of them would be the greatest.* *Luke 9:46* (NIV)

One would think that after being with Jesus for three-plus years that His disciples would not be arguing with one another, particularly when it came to having power and authority. This was not an isolated event.

> *A dispute also arose among them as to which of them was considered to be greatest.*
>
> *Luke 22:24* (NIV)

This dispute happened in the upper room during the final meal with His disciples, mere hours before His arrest and execution! Moreover, Luke wasn't the only person to write of prideful conflict among the followers of Jesus; both Mark and Matthew did so.

> *Then James and John, the sons of Zebedee, came to Him. "Teacher," they said, "we want you to do for us whatever we ask." "What do you want me to do for you?" he asked. They replied, "Let one of us sit at your right and the other at your left in your glory."*
>
> *Mark 10:35-37* (NIV)

Beyond James and John, all of Jesus' disciples believed the Chosen One would come and overthrow the Roman occupation of Israel. The Messiah would sit on a throne and rule over Israel with absolute power. His disciples – especially James and John – wanted to sit next to Him on thrones, thereby being the greatest among them. According to Matthew's account, even their mom got involved.

> *Then the mother of Zebedee's sons came to Jesus with her sons and, kneeling down, asked a favor of him. "What is it you want?" he asked. She said, "Grant that one of these two sons of mine may sit at your right and the other at your left in your kingdom."* *Matthew 20:20-21* (NIV)

The mother of James and John wanted what was best for her sons, at least in her thinking, and that was for them to be seated in places of honor beside the Messiah. People were blinded by ambition, and even those who were closest to Jesus had a thirst for power. Why? Deep within our sinful nature is our constant struggle with pride. Not once, but twice in the Gospel of Luke, Jesus told His followers the result of living lives characterized by pride or humility.

> *For all those who exalt themselves will be humbled, and those who humble themselves will be exalted.*
>
> *Luke 14:11* (NIV)

> *I tell you that this man, rather than the other, went home justified before God. For all those who exalt themselves will be humbled, and those who humble themselves will be exalted.*
>
> *Luke 18:14* (NIV)

Why did Jesus confront their pride? He knew "pride goes before destruction, a haughty spirit before a fall" (Prov. 16:18 NIV).

In the ancient world then, and in the modern world now, life is about image: title, wealth, power, prestige, possessions. Humility is wrongly confused with humiliation; yet in both Hebrew and

Greek, the word humility means "low, low to the ground." Humility means to willingly "go to a lower place." Jesus set for us the finest example of doing so when "he humbled himself by becoming obedient to death – even death on a cross" (Phil. 2:8).

Move into Humility

For elders and deacons to be at their best relationally, it is essential for them to individually call out pride in their lives, just as Jesus did with His followers. Moreover, elders and deacons need to move into humility.

> *In your relationships with one another, have the same mindset as Christ Jesus:*
>
> *Who, being in very nature God,*
> *did not consider equality with God something to*
> *be used to his own advantage;*
> *rather, he made himself nothing*
> *by taking the very nature of a servant,*
> *being made in human likeness.*
> *And being found in appearance as a man,*
> *he humbled himself*
> *by becoming obedient to death—*
> *even death on a cross!*
>
> *Philippians 2:5-8* (NIV)

Jesus journeyed into humility. He did not demand to be equal with God. Letting go of His positional authority, Jesus "humbled Himself," leaving Heaven behind and coming to earth below, Jesus "did not come to be served, but to serve, and to give his life as a ransom for many" (Mk. 10:45, NIV). Jesus put the needs of others before His own. Humility is thinking more highly of others than we do of ourselves (Phil. 2:3-4). Humility is not something done to us, but by us. Humility is not thinking less of ourselves but thinking less often of ourselves. It is a journey.

Even though Jesus was fully and completely God, He was born into and confined by a human body. Not only was He born to a peasant girl from an obscure village with a blue-collar carpenter stepdad and laid in an animals' feeding trough; He entered this world on a journey into humility, and that journey continued. He did not own a home, write a book, grow a business or amass wealth. Even in His death, Jesus moved into humility. He allowed Himself to be arrested, stand trial as a common criminal, and to die for sins He did not commit. Crucifixion was and is both horrific and humiliating. Hanging naked on the cross, the Roman soldiers gambled for the clothing He had worn only moments earlier; once dead, He was buried in a borrowed tomb. Jesus journeyed into humility, and if elders and deacons do the same, their relationships will be at their best.

Humbly Speak

For the Son of Man came to seek and to save the lost.

Luke 19:10 (NIV)

The phrase "Son of Man" appears over one hundred times in the entire Bible, and more than twenty of those references were Jesus' in His final days before the cross. Though the Jews, Satan, demons, and even a Roman centurion all declared that Jesus was the Son of God, Jesus did not refer to Himself as such. The title Son of Man clearly indicates a lowly, humble position. Jesus consistently referred to Himself as the Son of Man because He was secure in His identity. Jesus, who was the Son of God, became the Son of Man (i.e., born physically, putting on flesh; John 1:14). Jesus referred to Himself as the Son of Man because He knew that He was the Son of God. His identity was secure in

God. Jesus humbled Himself, and then God exalted Jesus, giving Him "the name that is above every name" (Phil. 2:9, NIV). After all, "those who exalt themselves will be humbled, and those who humble themselves will be exalted."

Do we humbly speak about ourselves? Like Jesus, are we secure in our identity? If not, we will struggle with self-esteem – building ourselves up with words that honor us but diminish others. We will condemn others while commending ourselves. Yet, if we are secure in our identity as children of God, we will speak of ourselves with humility.

Humbly Submit Over and again, Jesus called God His Father. Whether directly speaking to God or speaking about God, Jesus consistently and repeatedly called Him His Father. There was only one time when Jesus called God something other than His Father, and that was while on the cross when Jesus cried out, "My God, My God, why have you forsaken Me?" There are more than 160 references in the Gospels of Jesus referring to God as His Father, yet Jesus was fully and completely God. The Apostle Paul said, "For in Christ all the fullness of the Deity lives in bodily form" (Col. 2:9). Jesus was in complete submission to His Father.

> *After Jesus said this, he looked toward heaven and prayed: "Father, the hour has come. Glorify your Son that Your Son may glorify You. … I have brought you glory on earth by finishing the work you gave me to do."* *John 17: 1,4* (NIV)

Though fully and completely God, Jesus humbly submitted Himself to God. Jesus willingly and deliberately put Himself under the authority of God, calling God "Father" and respecting His Father's authority. Jesus submitted by walking sixty miles to be immersed by John. Jesus submitted to His earthly parents. At the end of this final walk to Jerusalem, He rode into Jerusalem on the back of a donkey, fulfilling Zechariah 9:9, "See, your king comes to you, righteous and victorious, lowly and riding on a donkey…" When we look carefully, we see His consistent humility.

We follow Him – so can people see humility in us?

It is essential for lead servants – deacons – to humbly submit to the elders of their congregation. Deacons serve at the request of their elders, and just as Jesus came to serve and not be served (Mk. 10:45), lead servants must have the same desire. They do not share leadership authority alongside the elders as peers among peers; instead, they humbly submit to the authority of the elders. Moreover, elders must not have an arrogant attitude towards lead servants, but one of Christlikeness; Jesus washed the feet of His followers. When elders and servants "submit to one another out of reverence for Christ" (Eph. 5:21, NIV), not only will people see humility in those church leaders, but the relational health between them begins to flourish. When elders and deacons choose to speak with increasing humility, they do so out of the overflow of their hearts (Matt. 12:34). When the interior world of each elder and deacon moves increasingly into humility, both speech and actions begin to reflect the person of Jesus Christ.

A pufferfish inflates, swelling its stomach to several times its normal size to deter predators. They metabolize a toxin that is foul tasting and potentially deadly to other fish. To humans, it is 1,200 times more lethal than cyanide. There is enough poison in one pufferfish to kill thirty adults. Like these fish, we can swell up with pride, making us look bigger than we are; and pride is toxic to elders and deacons serving the local church. The late

Bible scholar John Stott said, "Pride is your greatest enemy, humility is your greatest friend."[79]

Let each of us resolve to be at our best with one another.

What five words describe the relationship between your elders and deacons?

Given the ABCs of Striving, which one is most relevant to your congregation?

Given the ideas in the Thrive section, which one is most relevant to your congregation?

What needs to stop and what needs to start to improve relations between elders and deacons?

---

[79] http://www.cslewisinstitute.org/Pride_and_Humility_SinglePage accessed Feb 11, 2020

Chapter 8: Deacons & Staff at their Best

Gary Johnson

As a pre-teen, do you remember waking up in the middle of the night because your legs ached? Our parents told us, "You have growing pains." As we physically left behind childhood and grew into adolescence, our knees and thighs would hurt, perhaps an elbow or both would ache. We were confused about such aches and pains. Our gray-haired grandparents, then, had growing-older pains. Having aches and pains makes some sense in a way. But childhood should be fun, not painful. How confusing.

In a similar way, a local church experiences growing pains, and when that happens, it is more than confusing. As churches grow numerically, changes occur. For many people, change is difficult to endure and manage. Growing pains can be felt in many ways: crowded pews and parking, more people but not necessarily more volunteers or more dollars, increased activity and expenses, and so on. Just as growing pains awaken a child from sleep, growing pains in a church can be a wake-up call that something is wrong.

In the previous chapter, we explored the need for elders and deacons to be at their best with one another. Yet, all too often, we noted that because of attitudes, behaviors and poor communication, elders and servants find themselves in conflict with one another, and the same happens relationally between volunteer servant leaders and staff. When a church grows numerically, growing pains occur in the relationship between servants and staff – and it is confusing.

Growing Pains Cause Confusion

When a church has fewer people on staff, the church depends on volunteers to lead in different ministry areas (i.e., care for the building and grounds, children and student ministry, guest services, teaching, etc.). These volunteers are often referred to as deacons, and some of them lead the ministry team in their area of giftedness. It is common for churches to use a democratic model for the internal structure of the church. People are nominated to an office, such as that of deacon, and those individuals are elected to serve on the church board for a stated term. These deacons serve as the leader of their given area of responsibility.

For example, a deacon may be on the church board and be responsible for worship. It is likely that this deacon is gifted musically and volunteers to craft and lead worship, recruit volunteer musicians and vocalists, recruit and train technicians, etc. This servant spends hundreds of hours picking out music, creating digital presentations, rehearsing the band and singers, as well as leading musically on Sunday mornings.

Yet, as the church grows numerically, the congregation becomes financially able to hire a worship minister. Once that individual joins the church staff, there is instant confusion between the volunteer leading the worship ministry and the newly hired worship minister. Think of the confusion at the first church board meeting they attend. Who is in charge? Who presents the ministry report to the board members? Who is responsible for doing what? Does the new worship minister craft and lead worship, rehearse the musicians, oversee worship technicians, and more? If so, does the volunteer servant ride off into the proverbial sunset, suddenly unneeded by the church? This growing pain has suddenly caused confusion.

If the elders and senior minister are not careful, this situation, and others like it, can become difficult. Unresolved confusion can easily grow into relational conflict. When leading volunteers (i.e., deacons) no longer feel valued, needed or wanted, one of two responses typically occur. One, the individual will find another way to use his or her spiritual gifts. In this example, a musically gifted leader who is no longer needed to lead the ministry team may go to another church to help lead worship. Or second, the individual may remain in the church but refuse to be of help in another worship-related role. Role confusion can give birth to relational conflict between servants and staff.

This is just one of the many ways in which staff and lead servants can be at odds with one another. Children or spouses of servants can be involved with ministries being led by a staff member, and when something unhealthy happens in that ministry area, a not-so-pleasant ripple effect may occur. The deacon may resent any hardship caused to his or her family member by someone on staff. Remember, servants are men and women ministering in the name of the Lord, just as the staff are men and women serving the Lord. These roles are highly similar with only one difference, the significance of which <u>cannot</u> be overstated: one individual is paid for his or her service, the other is not.

A Winning Formula

How can we foster healthy and helpful relationships between deacons and staff? An individual in the book of Acts provides for us a winning formula for doing so, and his name was Apollos.

> *Meanwhile a Jew named Apollos, a native of Alexandria, came to Ephesus. He was a learned man, with a thorough knowledge of the Scriptures. He had been instructed in the way of the Lord, and he spoke with great fervor and taught about Jesus accurately, though he knew only the baptism of John. He began to speak boldly in the synagogue. When Priscilla and Aquila heard him, they invited him to their home and explained to him the way of*

> *God more adequately. When Apollos wanted to go to Achaia, the brothers and sisters encouraged him and wrote to the disciples there to welcome him. When he arrived, he was a great help to those who by grace had believed. For he vigorously refuted his Jewish opponents in public debate, proving from the Scriptures that Jesus was the Messiah.*
>
> *Acts 18:24-28* (NIV)

This powerful story shows us three essential elements for healthy and robust relationships between deacons and staff: ability, humility and flexibility.

Ability: Notice in the text that Apollos was a native of Alexandria, a leading city in the Roman Empire. Established and named after Alexander the Great in 332 BC, the emperor placed a large colony of Jews in the city, and it is estimated that Alexandria had, at the time, the largest concentrated population of Jews outside of Israel. Moreover, Alexandria was considered an intellectual hub of the world with the then-largest library in the world with hundreds of thousands of manuscripts. The *Septuagint* (i.e., the Hebrew Old Testament translated into Greek) was produced in Alexandria. It is also known as *LXX* for the seventy-some Jewish scholars who translated this work. It was in this richly academic and scholarly environment that Apollos was born and raised. Apollos would have learned from the most educated of rabbis who taught in the enormous synagogue in Alexandria.

The text refers to Apollos as a "learned man," and says he had a "thorough knowledge of the Scriptures." Moreover, he had been "instructed" about Jesus the Messiah, of whom Apollos spoke "accurately" and "with great fervor." These words and phrases indicate that Apollos was gifted, skilled and formally trained.

This passage describes Apollos as a man who had the ability to lead and the capacity to serve in the body of Christ.

For deacons and staff to be at their best in relationship, they must take note of the ability that people have, particularly those on the staff who serve in the same ministry areas as the deacons. Those on staff may have invested time, energy and financial resources to obtain educational training for a sacred vocation in ministry. Staff members may have been set apart and ordained into sacred vocation following a calling of the Lord into ministry. Like Apollos, those on the church staff may bring exceptional skill and aptitude to the ministry team. Their ability is to be welcomed and appreciated.

Humility: Notice also in the text that Apollos was teachable in spirit. Though he was highly trained and well-taught, he did not have a monopoly on knowledge as "he knew only the baptism of John." Proverbial blanks had to be filled in for Apollos and that was noticed by the husband and wife ministry team of Priscilla and Aquilla, who were tentmakers like Paul (Acts 18:3). More than likely, they lived in a tent as they made tents. This couple invited Apollos into their home – probably a tent – to teach him "the way of God more adequately." He accepted. Though he wasn't learning from credentialed and renowned rabbis in a world-famous synagogue, Apollos was teachable in spirit because he was humble in heart. He was willing to learn from a man and his wife while sitting in their tent.

Humility is a God-honoring prerequisite for deacon and staff relationships to flourish. Humility is an attitude of the heart. It is how we think, and how we think determines how we live. If we think with humility, there is every greater likelihood that we will live humble lives. The words we speak and the actions we take will be rooted in humility.

Staff must be authentically humble men and women of God. Having academic credentials and ordination certificates on the wall do not permit them to serve and lead in arrogant ways. Like Jesus, staff must be willing to wash the feet of others (John 13:15). Like Apollos, staff members should be quick to admit that they do not know all there is to know about ministry. Like Apollos, there are proverbial blanks to fill, and there may be volunteers (i.e., deacons) in the church able and willing to teach staff members about ministry.

Similarly, deacons must think and act with the humility of Christ. Both confusion and conflict can result when, and if, lead servants are displaced from leadership roles by church staff. Like Apollos, volunteers (i.e., deacons) should model humility and they also need to be teachable in spirit. Deacons could learn how to serve more effectively in their ministry area from formally trained staff.

In his book *Humilitas*, John Dickson tells a remarkable story of famed mountaineer Sir Edmund Hillary. In 1953, Hillary, with his friend and Sherpa Tenzin Norgay, were the first humans to stand on the summit of Mount Everest. Along with being knighted, Hillary received awards, titles, recognition and fame the world over. Though he became known and respected by even some of the most powerful leaders, Hillary maintained a genuine spirit of humility. Dickson captured one such moment.

> *On one of his many trips back to the Himalayas he was spotted by a group of tourist climbers. They begged for a photo with the great man, and Hillary obliged. They handed him an ice pick so he would look the part and set up for the photograph. Just then another climber passed the group and, not recognizing the man at the centre, strode up to Hillary saying, "Excuse me, that's not how you hold an ice pick. Let me show you." Everyone stood*

> *around in amazed silence as Hillary thanked the man, let him adjust the pick, and happily went on with the photograph. It doesn't matter how experienced that other climber was; his greatness was diminished by this intrusive presumption. We are repelled by pride. Edmund Hillary's greatness, however, is somehow enhanced by this humility.*[80]

Flexibility: The text reveals that Apollos wanted to go to Corinth, the capital city of the region of Achaia. Paul had previously been in Corinth where he heard from the Lord in a vision: "Do not be afraid; keep on speaking, do not be silent" (Acts 18:9, NIV). Paul was intimidated and exhausted. This second missionary journey was both demanding and difficult, and Apollos became a part of the team at just the right time. After Paul left Corinth, he traveled to a variety of places to encourage believers (Acts 18:18-23). This was the beginning of Paul's third and final missionary journey. While Paul moved from place to place, Apollos was beginning his work of doing the same.

Deacons and staff need to look over the landscape of ministry in the local church and determine where they can be of help. A spirit of flexibility is essential if relationships between deacons and staff are to be at their best. Jesus came to serve, not be served (Mark 10:45), and we follow His example. After all, if we claim to be His followers, we must live as Jesus lived (1 John 2:6). An effective servant of the Lord is flexible and desires to help wherever he or she can in order to help ministry thrive and to be robust. This attitude will produce behavior that honors God. If staff members refuse to help in other areas of ministry outside of their job description, what kind of team member are they? If

---

[80] John Dickson, *Humilitas* (Zondervan, 2011), 70-71.

servants refuse to help in areas of need different from their typical responsibilities, what kind of team member are they? A winning team is made up of players who will not only play their position but will take to the court or field when the coach deems it necessary, such as when other players are injured. Flexibility that leads to availability is essential for deacons and staff to serve well with one another.

Taking the First Step

To implement the winning formula of ability, humility and flexibility, it may be necessary to take the first step towards a member of the staff or towards a deacon in the church. Someone must choose to walk across the room to talk. Someone must pick up the phone and initiate a conversation. To begin moving in the direction of improved relationships between staff and deacons, first steps are necessary. Perhaps that first step will be enabled by approaching God in prayer for a change of heart.

Spanish priest and theologian Ignatius of Loyola (1491-1556) is known to have said this prayer; a prayer fitting for each of us.

> *Teach us, Lord, to serve you as you deserve, to give and not to count the cost, to fight and not to heed the wounds, to toil and not to seek for rest, to labor and not to ask for any reward save that of knowing that we do your will.*

When have growing pains occurred in your congregation? What confusion resulted?

In what way will you take the first step and, specifically, toward whom in pursuit of better relational health?

Chapter 9: Deacons & their Family

Jim Estep

We are all part of a family. Regardless of the structure of our family or the dynamics within it, we live in the community of the family. We were born into one, grew up in one, and most start a new one. We identify ourselves in term of family: son, brother, husband, father, etc. While God identifies His people with many metaphors, He uses the imagery of the family to describe the Church (Gal. 6:10; Eph. 3:14-15; Heb. 2:11-12).

How does the notion of family, servants and the church all fit together? We really cannot separate our life in the family with our life as servants in the church. God wants us to enjoy our families. We draw strength from them, insights on life from them, and serve together with them. Lead servants do not stand alone in the church, but as a servant within their biological family and in the family of God.

Challenges to a Deacon's Family

All families, even Christian ones, face challenges. Christian families, endeavoring to set an example and live beyond the expectations of the world, perhaps find it more challenging, and perhaps most of all in the families of leaders – elders, staff, and servants. Without oversimplifying the requirement, the lead servant's family is to be a healthy Christian family. "Let [servants] each be the husband of one wife, managing their children and their own households well." (1 Tim. 3:12, ESV). A lead servant's family faces all the typical stresses, strains, and foibles of any Christian home; but there may well be some additional challenges due to their role in the congregation.

First, Satan loves fallen leaders – and servant-leaders. Lead servants have a very public presence both in the church and community. Dysfunction or disharmony in the family often distracts them from their ministry and tarnishes their witness.[81] Remember, your first responsibility is to your family relationships, then to the congregation.

Second, servants <u>are</u>, in fact, called to a higher standard. It is one thing for you to accept the call to serve the church; but with the acceptance of that call your family is also brought into the spotlight of the congregation and community. If families are not ready for this or were not consulted before you made the decision, they may feel unfairly drawn into the public view of others. Consulting with your family about your call to serve and minister as a servant leader, or asking them about it periodically afterward, is advisable.

Third, servants occasionally have to confidentially deal with difficult church matters. Anyone who has served in any leadership capacity quickly realizes they become aware of issues involving other individuals and families in the church, financial concerns, troublesome members stirring up trouble … and these cannot be shared with the family. One of the strains of serving in such a way is being unable to share with your family what you are experiencing. Families face the challenge of being kept out of the loop while one member – you – are part of the loop.

Fourth, servants assume the role of a servant to the entire congregation. Lead servants and their families often face not

---

[81] All families are to an extent "dysfunctional" because there are no perfect families. But, a genuinely dysfunctional family often doesn't recognize its dysfunction, regarding the unhealthy state to be "normal."

only the typical stresses of how work or community impacts the family, but church plays a more significant place in their life. Deacons face an additional set of responsibilities, those posed by the congregation, meaning that some family resources (time, money, etc.) are expended by you in serving the church.

Fifth, servants face the criticism of others in the church. Unlike people who simply slip in and slip out on Sunday mornings, who are, in a sense, innocent bystanders of the congregation's work, a lead servant is not. Servants often face criticism for what did or did not happen through or because of their ministry. The family of the servant can be harmed by collateral damage from criticism or conflict. To be healthy servants, we must be healthy ourselves, facing criticism and conflict head-on, knowing that we ultimately answer to Jesus alone, shielding our families from it.

The Dynamics of Family Relationships

While everyone wants to have a "healthy" family, often times we do not know its indicators, nor do we know the warning signs of dysfunctional families. As lead servants, we have to enjoy our family, which means we have to try to have healthy relationships within the family. Donald Joy, a family life ministry authority, has suggested that families exist in four different dynamic situations which he calls "family systems."[82]

Spoiler alert: three of the four are dysfunctional.

---

[82] The chart is an adaptation of Donald Joy's family systems found in *Risk Proofing Your Family* and is available, at the time of this printing, from him for just $13. Just send your request and return address along with a check or money order to Donald Joy, 1-5 Academy Drive, Wilmore, Kentucky 40390.

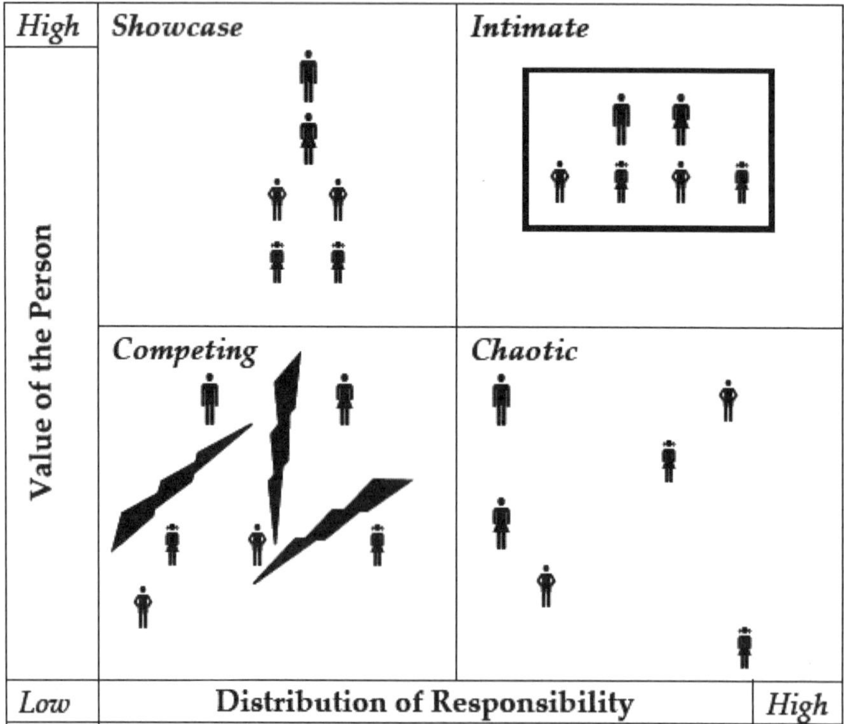

The first is called **Showcase**. In this dynamic, the family's relationship is dominated by a hierarchical model of authority, often favoring the male members. The chain-of-command progresses from father to mother to oldest son, to next oldest son, to oldest daughter, and so on. The Showcase family emphasizes their public image to the extent that cover-ups are common, and fault is usually attributed to non-family members.

The ***Competing*** family dynamic places low value on family members and distribution of responsibilities within the family. It is characterized by conflict and division within the family. Because family members relate to one another in a spirit of competition, compulsive behaviors develop. We have all perhaps seen a family wherein sibling rivalry is present, but what if rivalry extends among *every* member of the family? Each member of the family has a sense of superiority over the others, with one or two members of the family taking responsibility for maintaining the fragmented family relationships. This dynamic is characterized by a family that seems to have an angry disposition, seeming to operate in a state of perpetual tension and conflict.

The third type of family dynamic is ***Chaotic***. In these families the general rule is "everyone for themselves!" This is not the occasional load of undone laundry or the sporadic scheduling glitch; it is a relational landscape dominated by confusion and disorder. Little value is placed on members of the family; no one assumes responsibility for the family; there is no order or structure to the family unit. Hence, members use one another to fulfill their needs with casual disregard for the impact on other family members. Due to the low value of persons and the focus on immediate need gratification through any means, these families are characterized by a pronounced risk of drug or alcohol addiction in order to deal with the pressures of a chaotic lifestyle, as well as increased likelihood of sexual promiscuity in a search to find the intimacy missing in the family.

Naturally, the fourth option given by Joy is the ***Intimate*** family dynamic. As most may expect, it is characterized by a high value of family members, with *every* family member assuming some responsibility for the health of the family. In the intimate family there are defined roles, but without dictatorial command structures as in "Showcase." There are healthy boundaries in the Intimate family, the members know they belong, and relational ties are deep. This may sound ideal … and it is. The simple fact is that while the intimate family is ideal, no family is wholly in the upper-right block on the chart. Elements of the other quadrants exist within every family and manifest at different times. What is critical is that the *primary* dynamic reflects the Intimate family, with only occasional incursions by the Showcase, Competing, and/or Chaotic types. Intimate families don't just happen by accident. If anything, the Chaotic family is the one that simply happens. The Intimate dynamic must be cultivated by deliberately establishing and nurturing relationships between each member of the family.

Given the four basic family types, rank them in the order which they seem to be present in your nuclear family. What can you do to foster a more intimate family dynamic?

Rank	Dynamic & Comments
1	
2	
3	
4	

The Transitions of Family Relationships

We are not in this alone. Families, by their nature, are communal; they require more than one individual and are typically intergenerational. That means each member of the family contributes to the dynamics of the unit. Likewise, families face predictable transitions, but are often ill prepared to anticipate or move through the various turns and bumps in family life.

Jack and Judith Balswick discuss this parenting challenge in their book *The Family: A Christian Perspective on the Contemporary Home.*[83] By discussing the transitions that children precipitate in a family, the Balswicks note the change in relationship between

---

[83] Jack O. Balswick and Judith K. Balswick, *The Family: A Christian Perspective on the Contemporary Home* (Grand Rapids: Baker Book House) 2007, pp. 117-119.

not only parent and child, but between husband and wife, who are now "dad" and "mom!"

A Christian model of parenting leads to empowerment for maturity. The idea is that families are always in a state of flux because they are designed not only to bring the next generation into existence, but to launch them into independent adulthood as the child moves toward maturity. This process requires a family to transition through stages from newlyweds, to parents with all the demands of small children, to parents with maturing young adults, to empty nesters, then to mature, life-long partners. With the arrival of children, major changes occur in family relationships. I can remember thinking that I would never call my wife "Mom," but that happened while we had children in our household. That simple nomenclature change belied a greater, underlying change. It was a shift in thinking about our roles and relationships within the family. My wife is no longer *just* my wife, but also the mother of our children.

The Balswicks suggest that parenting occurs along two general axes, Parental Socio-Emotional Support, and Parental Control:

Parental Socio-Emotional Support

Relational interaction with child through discussion and dialog

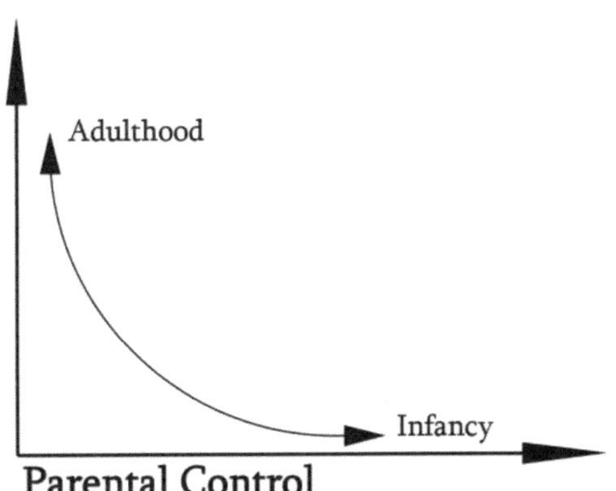

One-way communication
Giving direction
Providing unilaterally for the child

In infancy, the support dimension (the vertical axis as shown above) is low and the control (horizontal) is high. The child is dependent on the parents for everything, and parents are the providers. We do and should talk to our infant children, but it is not a conversation; it's more or less one-way. In early childhood and elementary age, the child is maturing, becoming less dependent on the parents; for example, they can clothe, bathe, clean, and feed themselves (bottles and diapers are gone). This calls for a change in parenting strategies. Parents increase the support behaviors, shifting toward teaching the child as the control aspect of the relationship begins to fade (the child is no longer dependent upon the parent for everything).

As the child enters adolescence this shift intensifies. While teens may desire independence, they are not truly ready for it, and they need to know they are being treated differently than during their younger years. Parenting continues morphing into a more participatory model of dialoging relationship within the family, with a continued high level of support, such as not only discussing life with the teen, but including them in the family's planning. For example, it was probably safe during childhood to plan a family vacation unilaterally, or to take the car in for two or three days of repairs. But teens have school activities (even in the summer), jobs, and other commitments. If they don't have enough time off accrued for a vacation, or they need the car to get to work tomorrow, but those plans haven't been discussed, they feel trampled when they haven't at least been forewarned. Teens are moving toward greater maturity, and hence the control dimension of the relationship diminishes as the supportive nature of the relationship increases two-way communication, bringing the teen into a quasi-adult status around the family table.

Finally, the child enters adulthood. Young adults still need their parents, but not as before, and once again, dynamics in the family continue shifting toward greater, deeper relationship. "Launching" a child off on their own is a major transition. It calls for a low level of control and probably even a low level of support, since they are probably no longer living in the family home, but in a dorm, apartment, or barracks.

Transitions continue, even after kids leave the home for independent adulthood. I remember calling my own parents one day after I had gone to college, and no one answered. I called, and called again, no answer. I began fretting that something was wrong. Finally, around 10 PM, they answered. Now *I* sounded like the parent: "Where have you been?!" "We went out for dinner and a movie." "You never did that before!" "Well, we do now!" A family is a dynamic relational context which we all comprise and to which we all contribute; there are no neutral bystanders in a family. Changes to our families call us to enjoy them in entirely new ways – first as couples, then as parents of young kids at home, and then as proud parents seeing them mature into adulthood themselves, and once again as couples, now enjoying the "empty nest" of senior life.

In which phase of family life are you currently? What challenges does it pose for you both as a parent and as a servant?

Being a Family in the Family of God

With the challenges faced by servants' families, and dealing with the types of family systems that dominate the American home as well as the inevitable transitions within the family; how do servants balance their ministry in God's Kingdom and still serve their own family?

Servants have to remember that their primary responsibility is to their family, not the congregation. The congregation will survive without them, others can rise to the occasion to serve as a spiritual leader, but a parent is irreplaceable in the family; no one can simply step into that role in your absence. If you have a family, a prerequisite to serving – specified explicitly by Paul – is that your family be healthy; don't let the service you render endanger the health of your family – which would then disqualify you from serving.

If servants' families are to be model Christian families, they do have to deal with image and expectations, but more importantly they must model how to deal in Christlike ways with failure, immaturity, and relational strain. In this way, the servant's family genuinely reflects God's family, the Church, when it not only models righteousness, but also forgiveness and care of souls.

In what ways is being a parent similar to being a servant? How does your experience as a family member aid in your service?

What family stressors have you personally encountered? Can you think of personal illustrations, or situations of which you are aware, that would illustrate any of these?

What challenges have you experienced in balancing your service as a deacon and your family life? What challenges face your role as spouse? What about as parent?

Part 4: Practical Applications

Chapter 10: Selecting Deacons

David Roadcup

As we consider the process of selecting believers to become servants or deacons, we must understand that the approach we take in inviting them to serve is critical. A good recruiting approach will put us on the road to great fruitfulness and success in building a qualified and effective servant team. Other, less effective approaches will produce a weak and inefficient serving team.

The approach presented in this chapter comes from over five decades of experimenting with multiple attempts for recruiting and selecting deacons and other servant positions. The approach suggested here is not the only approach. It is one, however, that has been tested and used repeatedly in various sized churches with excellent results. We will simply list the steps, one at a time, for your consideration.

Step 1: Understand the Need for a Plan

Traditionally, many churches have used the following process to select and appoint deacons:

- An item appears on the elders' meeting agenda which involves creating a list of potential deacons.
- Names are discussed and evaluated.
- People are assigned to contact those on the list.
- A minister or elder may see someone on their contact list in the hallway at church on a Sunday morning and, in the hubbub of the church hallway, invite them to consider this important role, or in a restaurant on Sunday after

church, someone briefly talks to a candidate about the possibility of serving.

- The question to the candidate might have been, "Your name has been suggested for deacon. Would you be interested in learning about the ministry of being a deacon and considering our invitation to join our Deacon team?"
- If the person is willing, a brief meeting is scheduled and completed, and the person joins the deacon team.

The problem with these approaches is that they are incomplete and ineffective. They will not facilitate a quality result. This approach is shallow and perfunctory. Remember the truism: "what you win them with is what you win them to." If the process for recruiting new servants to the church's ministry teams is done haphazardly, we will get haphazard service. The quality of deacons produced from our work is definitely connected to the way in which we recruit them. Using a well thought-through, tested approach will produce servants who make an impacting, positive difference in our church body.

Step 2: Identify a Leader and Selection Team

For effective servant selection, a specific person must be chosen to direct a Lead Servant Selection Team. A staff member, an elder or someone possibly with management experience from the congregation can do this task well. The Team Leader assembles their team of four to six people, oversees the process and communicates with the elders as their work progresses.

Step 3: Bathe the Selection Process in Prayer

Heartfelt prayer must be the foundation in this process. Multiple times in the book of Acts, the Apostles prayed and fasted before leaders were appointed. Prayer was a key to the choosing of the first servants recorded in Scripture. In Acts 6:1-7, we discover that the apostles prayed as part of the selection process (v. 6). Jesus Himself told us in Luke 10:2 that "The harvest is plentiful, but the laborers are few; therefore beseech the Lord of the harvest to send out laborers into His harvest" (NASB). Before Jesus chose the twelve who would become Apostles, He spent the entire night before in prayer, asking for guidance from the Father (Lk. 6:12-16). Serious, intense prayer should always precede the choosing of anyone who will lead in the body of Christ.

For what do we specifically pray?

- We pray for our Father to lead us to people whom He is calling and has prepared to serve.
- We pray for wisdom and discernment beyond ourselves – discernment which only comes from the Holy Spirit to lead us in this process.
- We pray for our Father to prepare the hearts of those invited to deeply consider this invitation.
- We pray for believers who are willing to accept this calling and step forward to say "Yes!"
- We pray for some who have been invited to decline the invitation, knowing that their availability or life situation is not conducive at this time in accepting this role. In the future, quite possibly, but not now. As we have heard in the past, "Sometimes timing is everything."
- We pray for the spouses and children of those being invited as they move forward in the recruitment process.

There is no better way to initiate the work of selecting servants than to seek our Father's face, asking for His leading and direction. **Please do not proceed without the elders, staff and Selection Team all bathing this important work in prayer.**

Step 4: Create a List of Potential Servants

The list of potential lead servants is created by the Lead Servant Selection Team. The Team works together in prayer, canvassing the leadership and the congregation for believers who would be good candidates. A list of names can be generated from surveying the people in the church body who seem to be given to service and leadership. Many believers with a servant's heart clearly present themselves as possibilities. Elders, staff and members of the Selection Team all provide input. Believers in the church who have exposure to a wide number of congregants can also provide suggestions. The Selection Team compiles a list and then submits the initial list to the elders. Note: this list is a list of *potential* candidates, recommended to the elders for their approval, not a finalized list of those who are going to serve.

Step 5: Meet in Person

With the elders' approval of the initial list, the Selection Team then organizes to make appointments with all candidates for face to face discussion concerning their interest and availability. This should be done in one-on-one or two-on-one meetings, meaning one or two Selection Team leaders should meet with each candidate.

When contacting potential candidates, we should not email them or use a text to invite them to become a deacon. Do not extend an invitation through a phone call. Also, avoid the "church hallway conversation approach." It should be a focused, face-to-face meeting, possibly in the candidate's home or over a meal in a quiet restaurant, or coffee together.

When talking with the candidate, the invitation should always be tied to and based on the vision of the church. Lead Servants who are called to support and labor for a God-given vision will be able to see the overall goal of the church and how their participation is connected to this vision. The team they serve on will join other teams to enable the health and vitality of the church to grow and flourish. Be sure to tie the invitation to serve to the church's mission and vision.

The discussion should encompass several things:

1. Address the topics listed below and any others you feel are important.
2. Provide the candidate the Ministry Application if the candidate wants to move to the next step.
3. Give the candidate a copy of the Lead Servant's Qualifications and Expectations outline and briefly go over it with them. Answer any questions they may have.
4. Ask the candidate about their availability to attend a Training Seminar coming up in the near future.

During your face-to-face conversation, there are several talking points that really must be covered in this vetting process.

- The candidate's spiritual formation is key to the whole process. How did they come to faith? What is their spiritual background? Have them describe the experience of their conversion and immersion. Ask them about how they have incorporated spiritual disciplines in their daily life (i.e. Bible study, prayer, Scripture meditation and memorization, fasting, etc.).
- What is their previous experience in the Body of Christ? Have they ever been in leadership previously? If so, what was the role? How did it go? How did they enter that role? How did they exit?
- Ask about their personal story and general background. What is their family life like? Do they have hobbies? How is their employment and professional life?

- Ask about their personal desire to serve the church. Is this role something they feel called into, something that they think they will enjoy?
- Share the expectation that every lead servant candidate must participate in an incoming Lead Servant Training Seminar. Will they be available? Share a date or two that the church's leadership plans to hold this seminar; remember to have this planned far enough in advance that the candidate will not feel pressured to re-arrange their immediate, near-term calendar to accommodate this expectation.
- Every church leader knows the importance of their spouse being supportive concerning a decision of this nature. This should be part of the discussion with the candidate.
- Before you end your meeting, it is important to share that you do not want a "yes" or "no" response at this initial meeting; at this point, it is only an invitation to consider stepping into this role of greater responsibility. The elders or Selection Team should feel free to add other pertinent questions to this list. This in-person meeting aims to ascertain the candidate's interest level, their willingness to serve, to answer any questions the candidate might have, and to encourage the candidate's presence at the upcoming Training Seminar.

Ministry Application A Ministry Application should be prepared and given to each candidate. This application is important. Doing so provides the Servant Selection Team with pertinent information concerning each candidate. Knowing the background and experience of each candidate helps in evaluating them as potential future lead servants. (A sample of such a document is included as an appendix.) [84]

Lead Servant Qualifications and Expectations Outline Every candidate being interviewed should have, on paper, a clear expectation about what their participation requires. An outline of "Qualifications and Expectations" should be given to each candidate. (A sample document is included as an appendix.)[84]

Availability to Attend the Training Seminar During the interview, it is best to mention that every potential servant needs to attend the approaching Lead Servant Training Seminar. At the conclusion of the initial meeting with the candidate, let them know that you do not want a "yes" or "no" answer at that time concerning the acceptance of this position. Ask them to discuss this invitation with their spouse (if married) and to lift the invitation up in prayer. The next step is to attend the Training Seminar where there will be a detailed explanation of the ministry position and how to execute it.

Step 6: Conduct the Training Seminar

The Training Seminar should be an informative and helpful experience. Information is shared about the servant's call, their qualifications and their coming ministry. All candidates interested in becoming servants need to participate in the Lead Servant Training Seminar.

---

[84] Our appreciation to Pastor Greg Marksberry and Thrive Christian Church in Lake Nona, FL and Pastor Tommy Baker and First Church of Christ in Burlington, KY for allowing us to use their prior work in publishing lightly modified versions of these documents.

Seminar Planning Details The seminar should comprise 3+ hours in order to cover pertinent information (New Testament word study, ministry philosophy of your congregation, etc.). The specific time allotment should be determined by the person who will organize and lead the training.

The Seminar is your "front door" into this vital role for your congregation. As your primary orientation and training event, offer it in a couple or few ways so that you set your servants up to succeed. This could occur weekly on a weeknight for two or three successive weeks. If planned far enough in advance, it could be a Friday evening to Saturday morning once or twice per year. Maximize the in-person participation, but don't forget to record this training and provide it on a USB, or posted to the church's video feed on YouTube or Vimeo (whether you make the link public or private). Remember, the entire purpose of this training is to encourage your new servant leaders as they are on-boarded in their new ministries, to make expectations clear, and to set them up to succeed in their new role.

Please remember: it is *critical* that all potential lead servants participate in the Training Session, either in person or virtually. This puts everyone on the same page with the same understanding and similar expectations.

Suggested List of Topics to be Covered Use training topics given below; add to these as you feel is needed:

1. The importance of the lead servant's role in the church
2. Biblical qualifications of a lead servant
3. A lead servant's personal spiritual life and growth
4. Characteristics of an effective lead servant
5. Lead servants' relationships with the church staff, elders and congregation members

6. The lead servant's ministry description and how to execute it successfully
7. The lead servant and his/her family
8. Lead Servants – heart deep in the church

Supporting Considerations Always distribute something to each attendee to encourage mental engagement and participation, whether an outline or a nice journal or notebook with the church's logo on the cover, etc. This allows for clear notetaking and enables those attending to take home information for future review. It can be a strong reminder as to the basics that were covered.

Additionally, it is always advisable to provide light refreshments for attendees to enjoy, irrespective of what day or time of day – coffee is almost always appreciated! If a meal is preferable according to your specific schedule, then plan a meal. Providing childcare may enable some to attend who otherwise would be unable, due to having young children at home.

Step 7: Ask for a Commitment

Soon after the seminar, contact each candidate by phone and ask for their "yes" or "no" response. Based on these answers, your new lead servant list is established, and it should now be submitted to the elders. **A word of caution**: *do not overlook* background checks on these new servant leaders. Once your candidates accept or decline your invitation to serve the congregation, a background check should be the final step before they actively begin serving. The well-being of the congregation is too important to skip this critical step.

The flow and timing of this approach allows for a specific invitation, surrounded by prayer, and a discussion with the candidate's spouse. It also provides a clear job description and training in how to execute the ministry into which the candidate is being invited. An overview of the ministry is shared and expectations are clarified. Then a clear invitation is extended and the candidate responds in the affirmative or negative. This approach "blows away the smoke" in terms of lack of clarity and misunderstanding of the servant's role.

Be sure to remember that how potential deacons are recruited and selected is a critical part of growing an effective and fruitful team of servant leaders. It takes planning, hard work and execution. But using this tried and effective approach will make this experience successful and build into the life of your church a part of important infrastructure which will greatly strengthen the church in fulfilling its mission.

What is your congregation's current selection process?

Given the plans outlined in this chapter, how does it compare to your current selection process? What is missing?

What kind of training does your church provide to lead servant candidates?

How does your congregation support and foster commitment from servant leaders?

Chapter 11: Equipping Deacons

David Roadcup

Two scenarios present themselves when it comes to equipping servants. Think of both examples here as new church plants.

"Main Street Christian Church" was setting up their ministry team system. They invited several believers to join their new servant team. The candidates were contacted, invited and attended a meeting where they were briefed on the work of lead servants. They chose the Ministry Team they wanted to join and were dispatched to their assignments. Several months after the church's launch, the Ministry Teams began to lose momentum in fulfilling their assignments. Some people were resigning their positions. Tasks were not completed. The purposes for which the Ministry Teams were created were not being accomplished.

"Second Avenue Christian Church" had a different strategy. They also contacted potential servants, had a well-prepared training event for them, placed them in Ministry Teams and then launched them. After they were launched, a staff member at the church stayed in contact with the new leaders and their work, encouraged them and provided listening ears, emotional support, advice and ongoing directions. Occasional training events were held. Fellowship dinners were held from time to time for lead servants and their families. Each month, a teaching article was sent to the servants through their email group, giving them new ideas and providing encouragement. The result was that the work of the lead servants at Second Avenue was fruitful and impacting.

What was the obvious difference between these two experiences? It was the continued effort to equip, train and support the members of the ministry team that made all the difference!

The Importance of Equipping the Servant Team

Every good leader knows the importance of continued training and development for those with whom they work. Coming to the end of His earthly ministry, Jesus, in His high priestly prayer in John 17:4, prayed, "I glorified You on the earth, having accomplished the work which You have given Me to do" (NASB). In a little over three years, Jesus finished the assignment given to Him by His Father. And what was that assignment? It was to usher in the Kingdom of God, bringing salvation to all. A large part of ultimately fulfilling His mission was the training of the twelve Apostles. Without equipping them to do His ministry, Jesus knew His mission would not be accomplished.

Jesus knew the importance of training and preparation. It was a large part of His ministry here on earth. He literally spent over half of His ministry time training and developing the twelve (some researchers say it was even more). Jim Egli and Paul Zehr, in their study of the gospel of Mark, determined that Jesus spent over 49% of His time with the disciples, and even more during the last several weeks and months of His ministry.[85]

Paul also taught and trained the believers under his tutelage. We know the names of a number of his learners. Timothy, Titus, Silas, John Mark, Aquila, Pricilla, Lydia and others were prepared for effective ministry through Paul's teaching and guidance.

---

[85] Paul Zehr and Jim Egli, *Alternative Models of Mennonite Pastoral Formation* (Institute of Mennonite Studies, 1992), 43.

Paul also makes the specific point about training and developing servants for the church in Ephesians 4:11-12. Verse 11 lists those who were to be the trainers (apostles, prophets, evangelists, pastor-teachers). In verse 12, he indicates these leaders were "for the equipping of the saints for the work of service, to the building up of the body of Christ" (NASB). The word for equip literally means to "to prepare, to equip, to make fit, or complete, to put into proper condition."[86] Paul is encouraging us to understand that all who will be effective at their ministries must be trained … and thoroughly so.

Big businesses spend hundreds of thousands of dollars every year training and developing their people. Sports teams and universities provide on-going training for their teams and leadership. The Disney Company makes this a significant part of creating success in their organization. In studying Disney, Tom Connellan wrote "My experience has been that companies that grow people grow profits. Companies that shrink people shrink profits. So look at the investment in human assets your company is making to be sure it's enough."[87]

Disney is a for-profit operation in the entertainment industry. Shouldn't we, as leaders in the Church, whose "business" is literally eternity, do the same for our people?

We cannot ignore this reality: both initial and ongoing training in any organization is absolutely necessary when it comes to seeing fruit and fulfilling the organization's mission. When

---

[86] Ralph Earle, *Word Meanings in the New Testament* (Beacon Hill Press, 1994), 312.

[87] Tom Connellan, *Inside the Magic Kingdom* (Bard Press, 1997), 140.

workers (servants) in organizations (churches) experience training and support, they complete their assignments.

One of the major hurdles over which many congregations trip is the lack of training and development for their volunteers. Whether those volunteers be elders, servants, small group leaders, youth workers or otherwise, quality training for ministry is, many times, very weak, sparse … or non-existent. The level of ministry we see from our servants (and others) will, in many situations, be exactly proportionate to how well they are trained, encouraged, and supported. One seasoned veteran of ministry observed:

> *If any church is to function efficiently for success in its mission, it must be guided by trained leaders in addition to the pastor. Opportunities for such training should be provided for all leaders in the church. A regularly scheduled training course for deacons is especially useful. Thus they can improve themselves and increase the extent and quality of their service.*[88]

And, putting a very fine point on it…

> *One of the miracles which God had worked in the church has been the progress which has been made despite the lack of trained deacons.*[89]

If we are going to invite believers into significant Kingdom service, it is only fair that we plan training regimens to equip them to serve with effectiveness.

---

[88] Harold Nichols, *The Work of the Deacon and Deaconess* (Judson Press, 1964), 93.
[89] Ibid, 94.

It has also been shown that effective training and volunteer care can result in greater retention of workers over time.

Lead servants are called by our Father to fulfill a very important work in the body of Christ. They are the first wave of workers who lead our ministry teams to do the foundational work of ministry execution. Without their contribution, the church would be crippled and unable to fulfill her mission. Because we, in the church, are involved in the most important work in the world, we need to do everything possible in equipping our servant team for effective ministry. Their equipping and the care we provide them is the foundation upon which their work rests.

Approaches to Training and Equipping Servants

There are key elements to the training, nurture and care of servant leaders in our churches. Below are effective means to train, motivate and increase their effectiveness.

Formal Training events are group events that convey quality information, instruction, ideas and inspiration to build up effective lead servants. These gatherings should also have a camaraderie and team-building aspect to them.

Such gatherings could be a seminar such as described in the previous chapter, held yearly, incorporating currently serving deacons around tables with the new candidates. This could also be a semi-annual training event for servants; perhaps a two-hour event for additional training, to refresh and refocus the servants of your church, to remind them of the vision of the congregation, offer new ideas and motivate them in their service. Gatherings like these are also the perfect opportunity to say "thank you" in tangible ways to these Kingdom workers. Bring in a special speaker physically or virtually to address them. This event should be centered on Scripture, prayer and helpful information for those attending.

Conventions, Seminars and Conferences are offered annually that would be of great benefit to servants. The major focus of a convention probably will not focus on the specific role of a deacon, but a well-planned conference in their ministry area (i.e. music/worship, children's ministry, etc.) can be a great benefit. Great speakers in main sessions, workshop presenters, and the networking possibilities can take attendees to a new level in their work.[90]

To maximize this experience, before the conference begins, why not contact one of the main speakers and ask that they join you and your team for breakfast or lunch while they are there? On many occasions, the speakers are very agreeable to meet with a team for an hour or more and interact with them. (Sometimes a speaker will ask for a fee for their time.) If you are able to make this arrangement with one or more of the speakers, be sure to have a list of prepared questions with which to interact with your guest. I have done this on several occasions with excellent results.

If at all possible, the church should budget the conference registration fee for your servants, or at least a significant portion. This is an excellent way to show appreciation to them for their work.

---

[90] There is a myriad from which to choose, but as a sampling: Renew, International Conference on Missions ("ICOM"), Exponential Conference, Catalyst Conference, Spire Conference, The Discipleship Forum, Center for Work and Faith Conference, Global Leadership Summit...

Encouraging servants to ***Read*** and add to their knowledge base is a healthy way to strengthen their faith and service. Books, whether in print or e-book format, are significant tools to stimulate their work. Help your servants to find helpful online tools like podcasts, articles, newsletters, blogs and so on to keep them fresh and aware of creative ways to serve.

Retreats offered annually can be an excellent way to communicate content, share fellowship and build relationships. Set aside a Friday evening and Saturday or a Saturday only to provide opportunities for further teaching of your servants. Be sure to conduct the retreat away from the church building to ensure a lack of interruptions and create a better focus for the event.

Show Appreciation to lead servants and other volunteers in tangible ways. Finding ways to say "thank you" is one of the best ways to "pay" those who serve. People appreciate being recognized and thanked. Phone calls, personal notes sent through snail mail, a text, a social media post, or just a word of encouragement in the hallway at church all deliver the message "We see your service and contribution to this church. You are appreciated!" After an effective year of service, why not have an Appreciation Dinner for servants and their spouses? At this dinner, you can give a small gift (book, coffee cup, etc.) to each of them for their service. Expressing appreciation is a significant way we recognize and bless those with whom we work.

Lead Servant Placement

The very best approach to placing a lead servant into ministry is to utilize them in areas of their giftedness, interest and passion. They will minister with much more impact through this approach than just randomly placing workers in open slots to be filled.

How do we discover the best placement for each worker? Scripture tells us that the Lord has placed in the life of every believer gifts and abilities to be used to build up the body of Christ (1 Cor. 12:7, 11). We attempt to identify the gifts and abilities God has uniquely placed in the life of each servant.

An excellent way to assess a believer's gifts and abilities is through the use of Spiritual Gifts Inventories.[91] Using an inventory will help determine where a servant should work with the greatest effectiveness. Many of these inventories are self-administered, self-grading and also, very accurate. The inventories can be taken at home and then brought to a one-on-one meeting or a ministry team meeting for sharing. It doesn't make sense to put a person in a role where they have no interest or gifting, and doing so will likely be harmful rather than helpful. Use one of the spiritual gift inventories for each servant to ascertain his or her best place of effectiveness.

Training and developing our servants is a major key to a healthy church and fruitful ministry. When we invest time, energy and preparation into training and nurturing our servants, we move our church and kingdom efforts to a new level.

---

[91] As with conferences, there are many spiritual gift helps available, both for purchase and for free. A sampling of books:
Finding Your Spiritual Gifts Questionnaire, C. Peter Wagner
Your Spiritual Gifts Inventory, Charles Bryant
Team Ministry Spiritual Gifts Inventory, Larry Gilbert
Discovering Your Spiritual Gifts..., Kenneth C. Kinghorn
What Are the Spiritual Gifts?..., J.D. Myers
The Spiritual Gifts Inventory with DiSC Personality Overview, Sandy Kulkin

On a scale of 1-5, how highly does your church value the equipping of volunteer servant-leaders (deacons)? Write down or discuss why you settled on this ranking,

How does your congregation currently equip lead servants? Is it effective?

Which approach mentioned in this chapter is the best option for your congregation? Why?

What obstacles hinder the equipping of servant leaders in your congregation?

Chapter 12: Assessing Deacons

Gary Johnson

Everyone has that one thing he or she does not like to do. From going to the dentist or seeing the doctor, we just can't seem to get the appointment scheduled. Then again, it may be that the one thing we don't like to do is cleaning the clogged gutters or the litter-filled car. This list is long, and somewhere on the list would be the unenviable task of doing a performance review; whether we are the one being reviewed or person doing the review.

This is particularly true in the local church. Only in recent times have staff performance reviews become relatively common. Even elder teams are completing annual peer reviews of one another, especially those elder teams with whom e2 works! Yet, when it comes to ministry performance, one team often overlooked and not reviewed is the deacon team. No matter the numerical size of the congregation, there are volunteers (i.e., deacons) that make the ministry of the congregation happen. Some of these volunteers have leadership responsibility over other volunteers. These lead servants should be evaluated from time to time. After all, we are admonished by the Apostle Paul to pursue excellence: "And whatever you do, whether in word or deed, do it all in the name of the Lord Jesus, giving thanks to God the Father through him" (Col. 3:17). In the name of the Lord Jesus, would we serve Him halfheartedly or indifferently?

Assessing others is a difficult and challenging responsibility of leaders, especially in the local church. A troubling review in a business can result in the termination of an employee. When a soldier has a sub-par, disobedient performance, a demotion in rank can happen. Students who perform poorly can fail a class and be prevented from graduating. Yet in the local church it is difficult to terminate, lay-off, demote, or even fail volunteers. Assessing volunteers (i.e., deacons) is a necessary and demanding task. If church staff or elders conduct the review, it can result in relational conflict with those volunteering to serve. When we worry over potential conflict that may or may not result from reviewing volunteers, we fear that the volunteers will resign and no longer serve on our team. Hence, we delay and even put off doing any kind of review whatsoever.

Round Peg – Square Hole

If we choose not to conduct any kind of a review with volunteers, we can, at the very least, make it likely that their service to the Lord is being accomplished by the right person doing the right thing with the right spiritual gift in the right way at the right time and for the right reason. In other words, we should work very hard to prevent the "round peg – square hole" phenomenon from happening.

Too often, we take the "warm body approach" and place people in positions of service without ever helping them discover or affirm their spiritual gift(s).

Many Scriptures teach that we have specific spiritual gifts. Peter wrote: "Each one should use whatever gift you have received to serve others, as faithful stewards of God's grace in its various forms" (1 Pet. 4:10, NIV). Paul mentioned various spiritual gifts in Romans 12:6-8 and in 1 Corinthians 12:4-11. Without digging into these Scriptures' depths to differentiate the types of gifts mentioned, suffice it to say that we should help people identify their gifting if we hope to avoid having a volunteer misplaced in an area of service; having a "round peg in a square hole."

Many gift assessment tools exist, whether in print form or in a digital format. The local church should intentionally help people discover or affirm their gifting by pointing them to gift assessment tools. If a church chooses not to use actual assessments, we can help people identify their giftedness by teaching them to ask a set of four simple, yet direct, questions of themselves. While thinking about the task they are doing as a servant leader, ask…

1. Do you enjoy preparing for the next time you will serve?
2. Do you enjoy this task while you are doing the task?
3. Do you look forward with eagerness to the next time you will do this task?
4. Do you receive positive feedback from those you serve?

How one answers these four questions can provide valuable insight about the appropriate use of his/her spiritual gifts. If we hope to improve the performance of our deacons/servants without an actual review process, we must, at the very least, make every effort to have the right person doing the right thing with the right spiritual gift in the right way at the right time for the right reason. Such intentionality can help move the Kingdom of God forward in remarkable ways. Think of how this helped accomplish one of America's greatest feats in space.

On July 21, 1969, Commander Neil Armstrong was the first person to step foot on the moon, and when he did so, he made a statement that has become known and remembered by millions to this day: "That's one small step for man, one giant leap for mankind." Catherine Thimmesh in her book *Team Moon: How 400,000 People Landed Apollo 11 on the Moon* (Houghton Mifflin, 2006) teaches school children that this mission was made possible because hundreds of thousands of gifted and skilled people worked together for this common purpose. At NASA's Kennedy Space Center alone, approximately 17,000 worked as engineers, computer technicians, military support, mechanics, contractors, etc. Thousands more worked at many other sites, producing materials, systems, and so on, that all came together in Apollo 11. More than five hundred people worked on the space suits alone, carefully sewing them stitch-by-stitch. This historical accomplishment was made possible by having the right people doing the right thing with the right skills in the right way at the right time and for the right reason.

Just as Thimmesh tries to teach school children of this fact, it is important that children of God learn and pursue this same truth in the local church. The Kingdom of God is effectively advanced when, with servant hearts, we work together to make Jesus the famous One in our place of ministry – and beyond.

Accountability is Good and Right

Many people give accountability a bad rap, when it is both good and right. Why is that the case? Accountability is biblical, readily found on the pages of Scripture. First and foremost, every person will someday be held accountable before God: "…each of us will give an account of ourselves to God" (Rom. 14:12, NIV). "Everything is uncovered and laid bare before the eyes of him to whom we must give account" (Heb. 4:13, NIV). People in the church are admonished to obey elders because elders will be accountable to God for the condition of the sheep in the flock: "…your leaders … must give an account" (Heb. 13:17, NIV). Even Satan is accountable to God. In Job 1:6-7 and 2:1-2, Satan appeared in the heavenly court, whereupon God demanded: "Where have you come from?" God held Satan accountable.

Accountability is a reporting-in to one another. We see an example of this in the early Church. The Apostles in Jerusalem sent Barnabas to Antioch (Acts 11) to advance the Gospel. Once there, Barnabas invited Paul to join him in the work. Then, in Acts 15:1-4, they returned to Jerusalem and upon their arrival, they "reported" to the apostles and elders all that they had done in Antioch and beyond. They made themselves accountable to those who were over them in authority. Even after training His disciples and sending them out two-by-two, Jesus had a moment of accountability with His disciples. Upon their return, they reported to Jesus all that they had done, speaking to the success of their mission (Mk. 6:7, 30; Lk. 10:1-20).

We need to teach and preach that being held accountable is both good and right, in relationships as well as in ministry performance. From staff to elders to servants, we should invite people to speak into our lives. We should want to live examined lives – for the express purpose of becoming more like Jesus. We will only review lead servants once we create an authentic environment in which people understand that accountability is both good and right because is it biblical.

When Sparks Fly

In Proverbs 27:17, we read, "As iron sharpens iron, so one person sharpens another" (NIV). When reading and thinking of this truth, it is easy for us to see proverbial sparks fly in our minds. When one person attempts to speak into the life of another, especially as in a performance review, the conversation can quickly go south. Sparks can fly, especially when speaking with a volunteer. To that end, when assessing the work of a servant (i.e., deacon), it is important to focus on three essential issues: attitude, behavior and capability.

Attitude: A servant's attitude is significant to the health and well-being of a ministry team. They must buy into the vision, mission and values of the team, and champion the ministry efforts that the team pursues and provides to the local church. Their attitude involves humility, servanthood, sacrifice, teamwork, respect of others, Christlikeness, and more.

Concert pianist Arthur Rubenstein (1887-1982) said, "You cannot play the piano well unless you are singing within you."[92] Similarly, an individual cannot perform well in his or her area of ministry without a right and good interior world. How we think determines how we perform. Pastor and leadership author John Maxwell stated: "When confronted with a difficult situation, a person with an outstanding attitude makes the best of it while he gets the worst of it. Life can be likened to a grindstone. Whether it grinds you down or polishes you depends on what you are made of."[93]

When attempting to review a servant leader's performance, his or her attitude about their area of service is of great importance to their actual effectiveness. When the volunteer champions the vision, mission and values of the team, affirm that individual's attitude. Indicate how his/her demeanor is of great benefit to others on the team, particularly when leading by example.

Behavior: Behaviors are born out of attitudes. How we think determines how we live or behave. Should a servant have a great, positive, healthy attitude, it will be reflected in their behavior and performance. He or she will be a team player, eager to serve and help in any way needed, looking for ways to help others on

---

[92] https://www.quotetab.com/quotes/by-arthur-rubinstein

[93] Maxwell, John. *Today's Christian Woman* (July/Aug 2003), 10.

the team to succeed. This person will build others up, encouraging and equipping them to be all that they can be for the Lord.

Similarly, if someone has a sour, negative attitude towards his or her area of service, performance will suffer. They will not think first and foremost of the team and its ministry, will do as little as possible, lack interest in becoming more proficient as a volunteer, be content with mediocrity, etc.

Moreover, Jesus said that our mouth speaks what is in our heart (Matt. 12:34). Whatever is in a person's mind (i.e., how one thinks) will be expressed verbally or even virtually in social media. If a servant has a great, healthy, and spiritually strong interior world (i.e., heart), speech will be expressed that reflects such a good attitude. Conversely, if a servant has an unhealthy interior world and is not in a good place spiritually or emotionally, that person will express what's reflected within him or her. Attitude births behavior.

Author and pastor Scott Sauls described the reality of attitude giving birth to behavior in the life of a nursery volunteer. Something remarkable happened when a mother named Janet dropped off her two sons in the church nursery.

> *After the service, while Janet was waiting in the nursery line to retrieve her boys, one of the nursery workers quietly approached her and said that there had been some issues. Both of her boys had picked fights with other children. Also, one of her boys had broken several of the toys that belonged to the church. In front of a room filled with other children and their parents, Janet scolded her boys and then screamed in a bellowing voice, "S—!" Deeply ashamed and feeling like a failure, Janet got her boys*

and skulked out of the building. No doubt, we were never going to see her again.

But that unnamed nursery volunteer called the church office that Monday and asked if I could check the visitor notebook to see if Janet had left her contact information. She had. I gave the nursery worker Janet's address, and unbeknownst to me, she sent Janet a note. The note read something like this:

Dear Janet, I'm so glad that you and your boys visited our church. Oh, and about that little exchange when you picked them up from the nursery? Let's just say that I found it so refreshing—that you would feel freedom to speak with an honest vocabulary like that in church. I am really drawn to honesty, and you are clearly an honest person. I hope we can become friends. Love, Unnamed Nursery Worker.

The nursery worker and Janet did in fact become friends. Janet came back the next Sunday. And the Sunday after that. And the Sunday after that. And eventually, Janet became the nursery director for the church. Later on I would discover that when Janet started coming to our church she was a recovering heroin addict.[94]

It is important to strike a balance when reviewing volunteers. The swinging of the proverbial pendulum should not weigh heavily on what the individual does as a volunteer. Always make room for the development of the servant's interior world. Life is

---

[94] Sauls, Scott. *Befriend* (Tyndale, 2016), 29-30.

not solely about what we do, but about who we are … and about who we are becoming.

Capability: The third and final area of review for a lead servant should be the individual's actual capability. Attempt to make an honest assessment of a servant leader's skill and performance. We always want to invest in people, and one such way is to help them become increasingly capable to serve the Lord well with their gifts. To make this investment of time and effort, we may have to create margin in our own lives to make a difference in the lives of our team members. We may have to stop doing what matters less in order to start doing what matters more. To accomplish more of what really matters means doing less of what does not matter as much.

For example, if we lead musicians and some of the instrumentalists and vocalists are lacking skills, increase their capability by providing a skills class or private lessons. If we lead a guest services team and volunteers are lacking in people skills, improve their capability by taking them to training seminars or by mentoring them one-on-one.

We live in a culture that plays it safe. Think of how risk-averse we are in American society. We install security systems on our homes – and cars as well. We have locks on every door and window and gate. We purchase insurance policies on our health, our lives, our homes, our income, our vehicles, our vacations, and even on our minor appliances. We have become so risk-averse that, when parting company, it's just as common to hear "Be safe" as "Good-bye!" We do all that we can to minimize risk in myriad ways, and again, how we think determines how we act.

Our risk aversion wrongly intrudes on how we think about our relationship dynamics. We think developing fellow team members will create emotional or relational strife and, being risk-averse, we ignore this good, right, healthy practice. There is an old saying that to get to the fruit, you have to go out on a limb. If we hope to lead a ministry team that is increasingly capable of serving in exceptional ways, we must take a risk, review each servant's capability, and create an appropriate development plan. When doing team-wide review and development, it can be full of fun, laughter and enjoyment.

We've Been Given A Trust

Paul reminded us: "Now it is required that those who have been given a trust must prove faithful" (1 Cor. 4:2, NIV). Servants – deacons – have been given the trust of advancing the Kingdom of God in their local church through their selfless ministry. As leaders, the primary resource available to us is the time and skill of Christian brothers and sisters, and being responsible leaders requires our diligence in stewarding and developing that resource. Assessing the servants who make ministry happen in our congregation can be gratifying, but we have to be willing to take a risk and do so. Stop playing it safe. Go out on a limb and enjoy the fruit that grows from the team's effectiveness, and praise God when it gives Him glory.

When you hear "assessment," what is your initial reaction? Why?

What kind of assessment does your congregation currently do with deacons (even if it is informal)?

How might you find value in assessing the service of servants in your local congregation?

If you don't yet have an assessment program, what would be an effective first step in starting one?

Afterword

Both as a sentiment and resolve, #BostonStrong was birthed on April 15, 2013. In the moments following the bombing of the 117th running of the Boston Marathon, people were mutually strengthened and encouraged by the sight of #BostonStrong. The motto quickly captured the hearts and minds of people not only in Boston, but across the country.

This resolve – and motto – is not new. In 2006, the United States Army ran the recruiting slogan "Army Strong." In 2007, vocalist Britni Hoover produced a song entitled "Country Strong." After the most intense hurricane of 2012 struck the US, Hurricane Sandy's death and destruction moved people to declare themselves "Jersey Strong." When Chuck Pagano, coach of the Indianapolis Colts, was diagnosed with advanced leukemia in 2012, the team declared their year to be "Chuck Strong." After a movie theater in Aurora, Colorado, and Sandy Hook Elementary in Newtown, Connecticut, were attacked by gunmen, those two communities resolved to be "Aurora Colorado Strong" and "Newtown Strong."

One could look at these many examples, and at others like them that have not been listed, and then ask: is it overused? Has the "strong" phrase run its course? Is it time to move on from this slogan? Even though it appears this slogan is ubiquitous, it remains in use. It is widely popular and powerful, helping people to persevere in difficult and challenging times.

As we lead the local church, there are cultural trends that make ministry more difficult and challenging. We live in a "post-truth" age with increasing numbers of people – including Christians –

denying that absolute truth is found in the Word of God. From Hollywood in the west to Washington DC in the east and at all points in between, widespread disrespect of Christianity intensifies. Evangelism has become passive and discipleship is often lukewarm. The next generation wants little or nothing to do with the Church. Consumer-driven Christianity thrives, while progressive Christianity increasingly rejects doctrinal orthodoxy. Churches struggle to maintain their impact, attendance, involvement and income, and when unable to do so, thousands of local congregations close every year in America. These challenges – and others like them – call for the local church to be *strong*.

Athletes work diligently to strengthen the core muscles of their body's mid-section. A strong core is essential to the body's stability and coordinated movement. Athletes in one sport after another focus on developing their core as it makes them perform more effectively. In the same manner, every local church needs to have a strong core of servants, men and women, who provide both spiritual stability and movement. Developing a strong core of servants enables the local church to perform more effectively, advancing the Kingdom of God in remarkable and tangible ways. If we can be of further help to you in developing this strong core, please contact us at www.e2elders.org.

May each of us declare our determination and resolve to be …

#DeaconStrong:
Men and Women Serving Jesus and His Church

Appendix: Deacon Application

[Church Logo]

Please provide answers via email or in a separate word processing document.

Please indicate:

- Date
- Full Name
- Contact Information
    - Mobile
    - Home
    - Work
    - Email
    - Best Means of Contact
- Marital Status (Married, Single, Divorced, Widowed)
    - If married, for how long?

Answer the following questions in short answer or essay format. Answered forms will be archived in the church office.

1. How long have you been a Christian?
2. Briefly describe your spiritual pilgrimage; when and how did you come to faith in Jesus, were you immersed during this time, how has your faith matured, what has God been doing in your life over the last year, etc.?
3. How long have you been a member here at [our church]?
4. If married, is your spouse also a member here? If so, has s/he been immersed?
5. If you still have children at home, please indicate their names, ages, and whether they have come to faith in Jesus as well.

6. If you were divorced, please briefly describe the circumstances.
7. If you have ever served as an elder, ministry leader or deacon in another church, please indicate the church name, your role, and when.
8. In what ministries are you currently serving here at [church name]?
9. Have you served in other ministries here in the past? If so, which ministries and when?
10. Are you currently leading a ministry here at [church name]? If so, are you willing to give that up and replace yourself so that you might serve in this new way?
11. To what ministry are you applying for Lead Servant?
12. What do you consider as your spiritual gifts? Have you taken a spiritual gifts inventory? How have you seen your spiritual gifts at work in the service of others?
13. Beyond spiritual gifts, what do you consider your personal strengths? Your weaknesses?
14. What is your view of the mission of the Church; how would your ministry role relate to it?
15. Are you currently part of a small group / life group / ABF?*
16. Are you willing to commit to attending our Servant Training Seminar and other important training events?
17. Do you currently tithe (or more) to God's Kingdom through the ministry of [our church name]? Are you more an owner or steward? Has your thinking in this area grown or changed recently?
18. Please review our congregation's core statements: vision, mission, core values [or priorities] and beliefs. Check the appropriate box below:

☐ I do not have any philosophical reservations or differences.
☐ I do have philosophical reservations or differences. (explain)

19. How do you view the nature of Scripture, its authority, authenticity, reliability, etc.?
20. Do you feel you are capable of introducing and leading someone to Jesus?

    ☐ Yes ☐ No

    What would be the key Scriptures through which you would lead someone in this process?
21. How do you handle conflict?
22. How do you respond to stress?
23. [Our church name] places a high value on servant leadership. Share your thoughts / philosophy on servant leadership.

With God's help, I am willing to commit myself to serve as a lead servant in this congregation to the very best of my ability.

____

Signature

____

Date

---

*ABF: Adult Bible Fellowship (i.e. "Sunday School")

Appendix: Qualifications & Expectations

[Church Logo]

Deacon Qualifications and Expectations

The HEART of a Deacon

Jesus is the Master servant leader!

> *The Son of Man did not come to be served, but to serve, and to give his life as a ransom for many.*
>
> *Matthew 20:28* (NIV)

Take some time to read and meditate on Matthew 20:20-28 and John 13:2-17. It is the expectation that all leaders at [church name] are servant leaders. We serve from our hearts as modeled by Jesus our Lord, especially as shown in John 13.

> *The journey of life is to move from a self-serving heart to a serving heart. You finally become an adult when you realize that life is about what you give, rather than what you get.*
>
> *Ken Blanchard, The Servant Leader*

Deacon Responsibilities

1. Directly report to the Pastor/Director who oversees your Ministry Area
2. Work with Pastor/Director to set goals and objectives for your Ministry Area.
3. Recruit other volunteers to serve with you.
4. Manage volunteers within Ministry to ensure their ministry responsibilities are effectively carried out.

5. Meet with ministry volunteers as needed, and no less than once per quarter.
6. Serve as primary resource person for volunteers in your Ministry area
7. Execute the budget designated for your Ministry area

Understanding expectations clearly is one of the key morale builders for any leader. Additionally, when we operate within boundaries, there is added benefit in the alignment and synergy of mission and resources. This leads to a powerful and effective ministry. Consider a river: it can power an entire city with electricity – or destroy that same city in a flood.

Guidelines for Deacons

- All activities within your Ministry Area must be in accordance with the Bible and the specific vision, mission, and values of [our church].
- Operate within the approved budgeted amount for the ministry you lead. Additional funds require the approval of [staff position] and your Ministry Pastor/Director.
- You may spend up to [amount / $500] on budgeted expenses with the submission of a [form name / "Disbursement Form"] to the [staff position]. Spending a budgeted amount over [amount] requires the permission of your Ministry Area Pastor/Director and the [staff position]. (This guideline is in place for cash flow purposes.)

Jesus never sought to lure men to Him by the offer of an easy way; He sought to challenge them, to waken the sleeping chivalry of their souls, by a way which none could be higher or harder. He came not to make life easy, but to make men great.

William Barclay

Expectations of Deacons

As a Deacon, I will…

- Support the Vision, Mission, and Values [or Priorities] of our congregation with enthusiasm.
- Actively participate with the Ministry Team to which I have been assigned.
- Have been a member at [our church] for more than one year.
- Give a tithe of my income (or greater) to God's Kingdom through the ministry of this, my chosen home church.
- Be connected in relationship with a life group / small group / ABF.
- Attend worship weekly unless hindered by illness, emergency, or unusual work circumstances.
- Work for harmony and unity in the church body, never allowing gossip or rumors to propagate and cause division.
- Attend necessary Ministry Team meetings unless hindered by work, illness, or emergency.
- Maintain confidentiality regarding circumstances and discussions.
- Fulfill my assigned responsibilities with diligence.

Paul listed qualifications of servant leaders in his first letter to Timothy, and we are introduced to the very first ministry leader qualifications in the early days of the Church, in Acts 6. In this 21st Century, we expect no less than our predecessors did.

Additionally, we at [our church] have the following expectations of the way that lead servants will carry out their ministries. We recommend that all ministry team leaders complete [class name(s)] which are offered periodically in our congregation.

Qualifications for Deacons

• Full of Wisdom and Holy Spirit	Acts 6:3
• Respectable	1 Tim. 3:8
• Sincere	1 Tim. 3:8
• Not indulging (i.e. substance abuse)	1 Tim. 3:8
• Not pursue dishonest gain	1 Tim. 3:8
• Keeping hold of faith / clear conscience	1 Tim. 3:9
• Must be tested	1 Tim. 3:10
• Nothing [found] against them	1 Tim. 3:10
• Faithful to his wife	1 Tim. 3:12
• Manage his children/household well	1 Tim. 3:12